OBAMA
A PROMISE OF CHANGE

OBAMA
A PROMISE OF CHANGE

David Mendell

Adaptation by Sarah L. Thomson

Amistad

Collins

An Imprint of HarperCollins Publishers

Amistad is an imprint of HarperCollins Publishers.
Collins is an imprint of HarperCollins Publishers.

Adapted from *Obama: From Promise to Power*, this is the story of Obama's
life from childhood up until his decision to run for president, including an
afterword about his presidential campaign through the Ohio primary.

Obama: A Promise of Change
Text copyright © 2008 by David Mendell

Library of Congress Cataloging-in-Publication Data is available.
ISBN 978-0-06-169701-2 (trade bdg.) — ISBN 978-0-06-169700-5 (pbk.)

Typography by Michelle Gengaro
3 4 5 6 7 8 9 10
v
First Edition

For my father,
whose enduring example of moral courage
has always shown the way

Contents

Acknowledgments

My literary agent, Jim Hornfischer, was among the first to see the promise of this project; his steady hand from the first proposal through the final manuscript was invaluable. Stacey Barney, the editor who purchased this book for Amistad, deserves my gratitude for her enthusiasm and foresight. Dawn Davis steered me through some difficult moments as this story unfolded and I am grateful to her. And Rakesh Satyal, this book's final editor, struck just the right touch of firmness and compassion, but I especially owe him for his patience with a first-time author.

I thank all of those in Obama's universe who allowed me to harvest their thoughts and kept me in the loop. Robert Gibbs, David Axelrod, Dan Shomon, Julian Green, Jim Cauley, Pete Giangreco, Maya Soetoro-Ng, Michelle Obama and, especially, Barack Obama, have my utmost appreciation. Many journalists who have written about Obama enhanced my observations about him, with Jeff Zeleny, Ben Wallace-Wells, Laurie Abraham, and Lynn Sweet at the top of that list.

At the *Chicago Tribune*, the number of my colleagues deserving thanks is innumerable. The short list: Hanke Gratteau, Ann Marie Lipinski, George de Lama, Bob Secter, Jim Webb, Mike Tackett, John Chase, Liam Ford, John McCormick, Ray Long, Rick Pearson, Pete Souza, Rick Kogan, and Flynn McRoberts and the Cypriot brotherhood. Jim O'Shea, now at the *Los Angeles Times*, gave his blessing to this project, and I thank him for that. Darnell Little deserves special thanks for listening to me drone on, day after day, as I collected my scattered thoughts into something that resembled coherent prose.

Many journalists and others also deserve mention for helping me climb the mountain to this point. Again, the short list: Steve Rohs, John Cole, Steve Bennish, Susan Vinella, Abdon Pallasch, Regina Waldroup, Armelia Jefferson, and Jim Bebbington. My good friends Mark Adams, Greg DeSalvo and Dave Doran helped keep me sane; and without Glenn Gamboa, this book would not have happened. Shawn Taylor provided early inspiration and encouragement, and I cannot thank her enough. Finally, the happy innocence of my son, Nathan, lifted me from the abyss at countless desperate moments.

1 Got Some Game

I'm LeBron, baby.
—Barack Obama

The swagger in Barack Obama's step appeared even cockier than usual on the afternoon of July 27, 2004.

Obama led reporters, aides, and a couple of friends around a maze of chain-link security fences guarding the FleetCenter arena in Boston. A former high school basketball player, Obama walked as if he were heading to the free throw line for the game-winning shot. Hours later, Obama would take his first steps onto the stage to deliver his now famous 2004 keynote address to the Democratic National Convention—the meeting where the Democratic party would pick its nominee to run for president of the United States.

Obama would not be chosen to run for president in 2004. He wasn't even in the running. But his speech would take him from being a little-known politician from Illinois to someone recognized across the country.

I was a newspaper reporter covering Obama, and I was wondering if his strut was something of an act. Would he really make a national name for himself here?

I slipped up to Obama and told him that he seemed to be impressing many people.

Obama, his gaze fixed directly ahead, never broke his stride.

"I'm LeBron, baby," he replied. He was talking about LeBron James, the amazingly talented teenager who at the time was wowing crowds and teammates in the National Basketball Association. "I can play on this level. I got some game."

I wasn't so sure.

That evening, Obama introduced himself to America. He spoke of his beloved mother's belief in a humanity that all people share. He declared that America is a land of good-hearted people, a nation of citizens who have more to unite them than to divide them, a country held together by a belief in freedom and opportunity for all. "There's not a liberal America and a conservative America—there's the *United States* of America. There's not a black

America and white America and Latino America and Asian America—there's the *United States* of America. . . . We are one people. . . ."

Democrats from many different states, many different races, had tears in their eyes. I heard myself speak aloud.

"Yes, indeed. Tonight, Barack, you are LeBron, baby."

But three years later, as Obama campaigned to win the Democratic Party's 2008 nomination for the U.S. presidency, there were questions: exactly how had Obama moved this far, this fast—and was it too fast? Did he have the experience and toughness needed for the White House? Was his mixed racial ancestry a problem, an advantage, or both? Could this young senator with an idealistic message survive the pressure of a race for the presidency?

And most of all, even though many voters were enchanted with Obama, would the rest of America trust this newcomer enough to make him the leader of their country?

2 Dreams from His Mother

I know that she was the kindest,
most generous spirit I have ever known,
and that what is best in me I owe to her.

—Barack Obama about his mother,
Ann Dunham

Barack Obama's first book, *Dreams from My Father*, begins with the story of a telephone call from a relative in Kenya who told Obama, then twenty-one years old, that his father had been killed in a car accident. He was shocked by the call and didn't know how to feel, mostly because his father had left Obama's family when Obama was a toddler. Obama often told close friends that he grew up feeling "like an orphan."

Separated from his father, Obama was strongly influenced by his mother. "I mean, she was just a very sweet person," he said. "She just loved her kids to death. And you know, [she] was one of these parents who . . . was the opposite of remote, was always very present and would be your biggest cheerleader and your best friend and had sort of complete confidence in the fact that you were special in some fashion." He once told a women's group: "Everything that is good about me, I think I got from her." In a preface to *Dreams from My Father,* Obama wrote, "I know that she was the kindest, most generous spirit I have ever known, and that what is best in me I owe to her."

Obama's mother's full name was Stanley Ann Dunham because her father had wanted a boy, but she led her life as "Ann." She was the only child of a couple originally from Wichita, Kansas. Her father, a furniture salesman, moved his family throughout Ann's childhood—from Kansas to Berkeley, California; then back to Kansas; then through some small Texas towns; then to Seattle for Ann's high school years. After Ann graduated from high school, her father accepted a job in Hawaii and took his family to their final home, the city of Honolulu.

During all these childhood moves, Obama's mother sought comfort in the same place: in the world of books. She loved to read, a love that she would pass along to her only son. She was such a good student that, while still in high school, she was offered a chance to attend the University of Chicago, but her father would not let her go because he felt she was too young to be on her own. "She was extremely brilliant. She read a lot, a very great deal at a very young age," Ann's mother, Madelyn Dunham, remembered. "She was into all of these heavy philosophers by the time she was sixteen."

Ann Dunham was sweet and kind-hearted. But perhaps more than anything, she was a dreamer who refused to see the flaws in people. "Her feet never touched the earth," her no-nonsense mother declared. Obama has said that his mother's ability to see the good in people is the quality that he most admires in her. It is also a message that he gives in his political speeches—that all of us are bound together as one, and if we are to do well as a country, then we must focus on the good we see in others.

In Honolulu, Ann enrolled at the University of Hawaii at Manoa. There, in a Russian language class, she met a Kenyan foreign exchange student named Barack Hussein Obama. He was twenty-three and she was eighteen when they fell in love. Sometime in late 1960, the two slipped off alone to the island of Maui and married. On August 4, 1961, Ann gave birth to Barack Hussein Obama Jr.

In the 1960s, marriage between two people of different races was rare in the United States, especially between blacks and whites. In fact, it was illegal in more than half the states. Ann's father, Obama's grandfather, came to accept his daughter's marriage. But Ann's mother, Madelyn, was not pleased. She worried about the cultural differences between Ann and her young husband. She was suspicious of some of the tales that Obama's father would tell.

Barack Obama Sr. was the first African exchange student at the University of Hawaii. After studying in London, he arrived in the United States in 1959. He was the son of Hussein Onyango Obama, a farmer and elder of Kenya's Luo people. As a boy, Barack Sr. herded goats on the family farm near a poor village called Kolego. He did well in a local school and won a scholarship to attend school in Nairobi before coming to the United States to study at the University of Hawaii. But when he came to America, he left a pregnant wife and a child back in Kenya. He had been married in a tribal ceremony, and he told Ann he had divorced his first wife. She later learned that there had been no official divorce.

After his marriage, Obama's father moved his new family into a small, one-story white house not far down a hilly, narrow road from the university and across from a small park. When Obama was two years old, his father won a scholarship to study at Harvard but did not have the money to take his wife and son with him. He accepted the scholarship and never returned to the family, leaving toddler Barack in Hawaii with his mother. Ann later divorced him.

3 "Just Call Me Barry"

*Every man is trying to live up to his father's
expectations or make up for his mistakes.
In my case, both things might be true.*

—Barack Obama

Ann Dunham got married again after divorcing Obama's father. This time, she wed an Indonesian man named Lolo Soetoro, another foreign student at the University of Hawaii. After spending two years in Hawaii, he returned to Jakarta, Indonesia. About a year later, Ann and Barry (as Barack was called) moved to Jakarta to be with him.

Barry played in rice paddies and rode water buffalo. He later wrote, "I learned how to eat small green chili peppers raw with dinner (plenty of rice), and away from the dinner table, I was introduced to dog meat (tough), snake meat (tougher), and roasted grasshopper (crunchy)."

For the first time, Barry saw poverty up close.

Beggars would come to their door. In an interview, Obama said, "I think [Indonesia] made me more mindful of not only my blessings as a U.S. citizen, but also the ways that fate can determine the lives of young children, so that one ends up being fabulously wealthy and another ends up being extremely poor."

Barry's stepfather, Lolo, had lived a difficult life, very different from the comfortable, middle-class life of Barry and his mother's family. As a soldier in New Guinea, Lolo told the boy, he would dig leeches from his boots with a hot knife. Lolo told Barry that he had seen a man killed "because he was weak." "Men take advantage of weakness in other men," Lolo advised his stepson. "The strong man takes the weak man's land. He makes the weak man work in the fields. . . . Which would you rather be?"

As Lolo preached the importance of strength and courage to Barry, his mother told him about moral values. She said that four things were most important: honesty, fairness, straight talk, and the ability to make up your own mind about what's right and what isn't. Just because other children are teasing a boy for something like a bad haircut, she told her son, does not mean you should do it as well.

Ann also told Barry about African-American history. She gave him books about Martin Luther King

Jr. and the civil rights movement, and played recordings of the gospel singer Mahalia Jackson. She filled him with stories about African-American heroes such as U.S. Supreme Court justice Thurgood Marshall and movie star Sidney Poitier. Ann also talked up the good sides of Barack Sr., telling Barry that he had gotten his intelligence and character from his father.

During this time, Ann gave birth to Maya, her second child. But after several years, she began thinking about how many more opportunities would be available to her son in the United States. There Obama could get a better education than Indonesian schools could give him.

And Ann had other worries as well. One day Barry had been out playing and cut his arm on a barbed-wire fence. Ann borrowed a neighbor's car and rushed Barry to the hospital. There, in a darkened back room, she found two men playing dominoes. When she asked where the doctors were, they told her that *they* were the doctors. She explained her son's injury, and they told her to wait until after they finished their game. Finally they placed twenty stitches in Barry's arm. Soon afterward, Ann made a decision—her only son belonged back in America.

Barry was sent to live with his grandparents in

Hawaii, where he was enrolled in the private Punahou School (pronounced POO-na-HO-oo). Obama's grandfather's boss helped to get Barry accepted there. His grandmother, Madelyn, had a job at a bank that helped pay to send Barry (and later his half sister, Maya) to the school.

In his first year at Punahou, when he was ten, Obama got an unexpected Christmas gift: a visit from his father. Those weeks were the only time that Barry spent with his father while he was old enough to remember him. Barry learned that his father had remarried and that he had five half brothers and one half sister living in Kenya.

Obama remembered only a few particular things about his father's visit. He was impressed by the way his father could catch the attention of everyone in a room simply by walking in, speaking in his confident manner, moving gracefully. But he remembered another moment as well: an argument that broke out between his father on one side and his mother and grandmother on the other when his father tried to stop Barry from watching a holiday cartoon, *How the Grinch Stole Christmas*. His father believed the boy had been watching too much TV and not studying enough.

Barry was beginning to realize some hard truths—

that his parents' marriage had failed and that his father had abandoned his responsibilities to the family. He was beginning to doubt the stories he had been told by his mother about his father's greatness.

"My father's absence in my life, it was just so complicated," Obama explained in an interview. "He went from being a goat herder in a small village in Africa to getting a scholarship to the University of Hawaii to going to Harvard. But he was somebody who never really achieved his potential . . . He was a brilliant guy, but in so many ways, his life was a mess."

By the time Barry reached high school, Ann had separated from Lolo and returned to Hawaii with Maya. The family lived in a small apartment just a few blocks from Punahou. "Hawaii was heaven for a kid and . . . I was sort of a goof-off," Obama admitted. His days were filled with hanging out at the beach, bodysurfing on the rolling Pacific waves, and playing sports, especially basketball—lots and lots of basketball. For Obama, Julius Erving, better known as Doctor J, was a hero—a gentlemanly, smart, and thoughtful African-American sports figure. Doctor J's dunks were wondrous to the eye. He seemed to fly through the air, effortlessly pinwheeling the basketball and slamming it into the hoop.

Most of Obama's friends were white, although in his book he describes long conversations with an older black friend, Keith Kakugawa, who had moved from Los Angeles to Hawaii. He described these talks as his first attempt to understand the complicated questions about race that were beginning to rise in his mind. Kakugawa said of Barry, "He wasn't this all-smiling kid. He was a kid that would be going through adolescence, minus parents, feeling abandoned. . . . He did have a lot of race issues, inner race issues, being both black and white."

Most of the teenager's white friends had no idea that Barry thought so much about race. Bobby Titcomb, one of Barry's closest high school friends, said he never felt that his friend was struggling to understand what his race meant for him. "He was just a normal Hawaiian kid, a normal guy," Titcomb said. "In Hawaii, you know, you have five best friends and one's Chinese, one's Japanese, one's Hawaiian, and so on. It is kind of just a melting pot. It was cool to have a black friend, you know. So I, you know, I never saw it."

Titcomb, however, did remember that Barry had his own style and personality. Barry had his own mind and, like his mother, never did what was expected just because it was expected. "When somebody was getting teased, he kind of gave that look, almost a look of disapproval," Titcomb recalled. "So that's kind of just the way he was. He was different in a way in that he didn't buy into the normal. He didn't tease kids just because it was the cool thing to do."

But out of sight of his white friends, mother, and grandparents, Barry struggled to understand what being African-American meant. "I was trying to raise myself to be a black man in America," he wrote, "and . . . no one around me seemed to know exactly what that meant." A small-minded tennis coach joked about his color rubbing off, so Barry quit the tennis team. He took two white friends to a party thrown by blacks and was angry to see how uncomfortable they were.

As a teenager Barack sometimes skipped homework and buried himself in the works of black authors: Langston Hughes, Ralph Ellison, James Baldwin, Richard Wright, W.E.B. DuBois. He felt most closely connected to the *Autobiography of Malcolm X*.

Barry had something in common with many African-American boys—he didn't have a father in his life to help him through these confusing times. He tried to mimic African Americans on television and in the movies. "So what I fell into were these . . .

15

stereotypes of black male behavior—not focusing on my books . . . playing a lot of sports," Obama said. He cherished his full Afro and could spend a long time picking at it in order to make it appear just right. The plastic pick would protrude from Barry's back pocket and he carried it wherever he went.

While Barry was in high school, his mother returned to Indonesia. But Barry was happy at Punahou and with his life in Hawaii. So he made an agreement with his grandparents: when his mother left, he would move in with them.

Barry was always a solid B student, but by his senior year, he was slacking off in his schoolwork in favor of basketball, beach time, and parties. On the basketball court, Barry felt most at ease. He learned a swift crossover dribble and a unique style of shooting, cocking the ball far behind his left ear and then tossing it toward the rim. His specialty was his left-hand shot from the corner.

But as much as Barry loved basketball, it did not always come easy. Punahou's team was doing well in his senior year, thrashing its competition, and finally the squad won the state championship. But Barry stayed on the bench most of the time, playing only in practice. His coach said that Barry accepted his lack of playing time and was a wonderful role player for the team. "I recall his sincere eagerness to want to get better, his positive attitude despite not getting as many minutes as he probably wanted," the coach said. "He was very respectful and understood his role."

But years later, Obama remembered, "I got into a fight with [the coach] and he benched me for three or four games. Just wouldn't play me. And I was furious, you know," he said, a twinge of bitterness in his voice.

At Punahou, Barry was popular among his classmates and teachers, but he didn't stand out. "All of the teachers acknowledged that he was a sharp kid," his homeroom teacher said. "Sometimes he didn't challenge himself enough or he could have done better."

Even if Barry was not a straight-A student or a standout athlete, some people spotted something deeper than a likable jock. Suzanne Maurer, the mother of one of Obama's close friends, said she sensed an energetic, ambitious spirit in Barry. "I recall that he was the type that if he had a dream, he would pursue it," she said. "The sky seemed to be the limit, and Barry was very much a can-do type person, even with sports, even as a benchwarmer."

The Mainland

4

Do you mind if I call you "Barack"?
—A female college friend

Hawaii was a wonderful place to grow up for Barack
Obama. Yet Hawaii can also feel far from anywhere,
a spot of land in the middle of an ocean. That peace-
ful solitude was both a blessing and a curse. Both
Barack and his half sister, Maya, longed to experience life beyond their island. In time, both would
make their way to the world's most important city,
New York.

Maya spoke of her brother's burning desire to
leave Hawaii to seek something—knowledge, adven-
ture, his own understanding of his race. "Hawaii has
ideas and cultures, and what have you," Maya said.
"But basically you felt cut off from the world. . . .
Here, I think he loved it here, and he was happy, and

he was well-adjusted—he was all of those things. But there were just so many big questions, you know, that couldn't be answered here that lingered. He sort of had no one to help him understand . . . for instance, when he felt someone was being racist or when he was struggling with issues of identity."

Obama wrote that his grandparents couldn't help him much with questions of race. And his half sister said that their mother didn't have much experience with the African-American community. Maya said, "Although she tried, she was not equipped to help Barack deal with what it is like to be a black man in this country. I don't think she knew at all how to help him. I think she just wanted to make him feel better. She was such a loving mother. She just wanted to make him feel like everything was okay."

Maya said her brother realized that he must experience African-American culture up close. Even so, after being accepted by several colleges, Obama chose to attend a small school in Los Angeles that had relatively few blacks on campus. Obama won a full scholarship to Occidental College.

At Occidental, Obama spent time with the school's small group of black students and instantly discovered that blacks in the United States were not at all the tough inner-city guys he saw on his television screen in Hawaii. They were as diverse as whites, with as many different points of view. "They weren't defined by the color of their skin, they would tell you. They were individuals," he wrote. "In their mannerisms, their speech, their mixed-up hearts, I kept recognizing pieces of myself."

Obama became involved in a popular campus movement of the day—urging the university not to invest in or do business with companies in South Africa because of that country's policy of apartheid (which means "segregation" in Afrikaans). Apartheid meant strict separation between blacks and whites, with most of the privileges and the power going to whites. This movement first taught Obama the power of words. "I noticed that people had begun to listen to my opinions," he wrote. "It was a discovery that made me hungry for words. Not words to hide behind but words that could carry a message, support an idea."

At Occidental Obama began to slowly drift away from basketball and partying. He practiced with Occidental's basketball team for several weeks but said basketball took up too much time. So he quit the team and instead played pickup games with students and faculty. Off the court and in the classroom, Obama found peers and professors who challenged him to think more deeply.

Rather than hanging out at the beach, Obama was now spending time discussing ideas in coffee-houses. Sometimes the talk wasn't always about the ideas, Obama admitted, but about impressing the women he met. "The schools I went to weren't driven by athletics," he said. "To get girls, you had to be the smartest guy in the coffee shop, not the best shooter on the court."

During one coffeehouse conversation, a young woman inquired about Obama's first name: Barack. He explained that it meant "blessed" in Arabic, and that his father's father was a Muslim. "Do you mind if I call you 'Barack'?" she asked. Obama smiled. And so the name Barry was put aside; Obama was now Barack.

One Occidental teacher played an enormous role in Obama's growth. Roger Boesche taught two classes that Obama took. The teacher vividly recalled a talk in which he urged Obama to work harder. He said Obama showed great promise but wasn't living up to it. "It was my feeling that his performance hadn't matched his immense talent," Boesche said. "I was pushing him, I guess, to develop that talent."

At one point, Boesche gave Obama a B on an

exam that Obama was certain deserved an A. "I knew that, even though I hadn't studied, that I knew this stuff much better than my classmates," Obama said. "I went to him and said, 'Why did I get a B on this?' And he said, 'You didn't apply yourself. . . .' And I was pissed."

Boesche and others helped Obama become less wrapped up in himself and more serious as he grew up. "There were people who recognized my potential and who were willing to challenge me on some of my less productive behavior, and I think that helped increase a sense of seriousness," Obama said. "Most importantly, it got me to recognize that the world wasn't just about me. There was a bigger world out there and I was luckier than most and I had an obligation not only to take my own talents more seriously but also to see what I could contribute to others."

Boesche's toughness was effective, and Obama worked even harder. Then, after his sophomore year, in 1981, Obama transferred from Occidental to Columbia University in New York City. "Occidental was so small," he said, "that I felt that I had gotten what I needed out of it and the idea of being in New York was very appealing."

In New York, Obama chose to spend time alone

in his apartment reading books by such writers as Friedrich Nietzsche, Herman Melville, and Toni Morrison, as well as the Bible. He began an exercise routine, running several miles each day. "I had two plates, two towels," Obama recalled. "My mother and sister, when they came to visit me, just made fun of me because I was so monklike. I had tons of books. I read everything."

"Those two years were extremely important for me," he went on. "I just stripped everything down and sort of built things back up. For about two years there, I was just painfully alone and really not focused on anything, except maybe thinking a lot."

Obama graduated from Columbia in 1983 with a degree in political science, the study of how different systems of governments work. He stayed in Manhattan and took a job with a company that published newsletters on business and offered advice to American companies that worked in other countries. For a year, Obama researched, wrote, and edited articles and reports on how to do business overseas. He didn't find the job exciting, and he barely recognized himself in suit and tie and briefcase, although he also had some dreams of being a powerful businessman. But this new vision of himself didn't match what he had always believed he wanted to be: a person who would "leave the world a better place."

Obama liked the idea of becoming a neighborhood activist, someone who would help the poor find ways to make their lives better. But he did not know exactly how to go about doing that. Finally he quit his business job and took a couple of part-time jobs in Harlem and Brooklyn that barely paid the rent. Meanwhile, he searched for full-time work. Finally he got a call from a man named Jerry Kellman.

Kellman was looking for people to work in a poor black neighborhood on Chicago's Far South Side. He wanted someone who would be a community organizer, to help people come together in groups to make changes in their lives, forcing governments, businesses, and landlords to pay attention to what they needed.

Obama and Kellman met in a coffee shop in Manhattan. Kellman was immediately impressed. First, Obama was black. It was hard to find a young, college-educated black man willing to work for the small salary that Kellman could pay. Second, Obama was intelligent and eager to make a difference in the world. For Obama, Kellman offered a chance to experience a new city and a new culture. He also offered Obama something more: a chance to be that person who would make the world better.

Later in his life, Obama would think back on his own experience, growing up as an African American. He would remember how his mother and grandparents, as well as his teachers and friends, had helped him turn away from some behavior—breaking rules, acting tough—that could have ruined his life. Too many black teenagers, he would say, are not as lucky as he was.

> When I see young African-American men out there and the struggles that they go through, then I connect with that. I know what that means. . . . I say to myself that if I had been growing up in low-income neighborhoods in Chicago, there is no reason to think that I wouldn't be in jail today, that I could have easily taken that same wrong turn. That is something that I am very mindful of and it is something that motivates me. Thinking about how you provide hope and opportunity to every kid is my biggest motivator. When I see my five-year-old and my two-year-old, it makes me weep because I see children who are just as smart and just as

beautiful as they are, who just don't get a shot. It's unacceptable in a country as wealthy as ours that children every bit as special as my own children are not getting a decent shot at life.

The community organizing job that Obama was about to take in Chicago was his first step toward changing the kinds of things he saw as unacceptable in the world.

5 The Organizer

He had this really refreshing dream and I was like,
"Barack, no, no, no. Not going to happen."
—The Reverend Jeremiah A. Wright

Barack Obama arrived in Chicago in June 1985, twenty-three years old, still idealistic about the goodness of human beings. But Obama's Chicago life would open his eyes to how complicated and unjust the world can be.

Chicago's South Side is the largest single African-American neighborhood anywhere in the country. In the mid-1980s, when Obama worked there, the South Side had both middle-class areas and neighborhoods of terrible poverty, where violence, drugs, and crime were part of daily life. Obama was interested in community organizing because it forced him into places like the South Side. He wanted to be closer to the real lives of those with little money and little hope.

Jerry Kellman, Obama's boss, cautioned Obama that his job would not be easy and that he should be prepared for failure. But if he concentrated on a few specific problems, he could make a difference. "All I had to do was to teach him not to be idealistic and he did the rest," Kellman said. "He was idealistic, almost ridiculously so. You know, it is in his nature. He was a dreamer. But at the same time, you can't perceive people through rose-colored glasses—right away, you have to get a sense of them."

"'Jerry Kellman is whip smart," Obama said. "One of the smartest men I've ever met." Kellman and Obama talked about everything from community organizing to Obama's vision for his future. Kellman urged Obama to get to know more people and to take breaks from what could be hard and frustrating work. Obama, who at first was spending most of his weekends reading books, finally took Kellman's advice. He started dating and had a girlfriend. But that relationship ended after a while, painfully for Obama.

Kellman described Obama as a man on a mission to help others. "Barack wanted to serve; he wanted to lead," Kellman said. "And he was ambitious, but never just for ambition's sake. It was always mixed in with a sense of service." Kellman saw Obama grow more comfortable as part of the black community. After seeing how Obama's political career turned out, Kellman made a bold predication: Obama would carry on the work of Dr. Martin Luther King Jr.

"Barack has become the expectation of his people," Kellman said, "and in that sense he is similar to King. As I know Barack, he will carry that as a weight, but he will carry that burden with great seriousness. . . . I think he knows that if he wants to go where he wants to go in politics, he has to speak for more than the black community. But I think the rest of his life, he will take on that burden of being that person who changes the situation for African Americans."

One of Obama's first discoveries about the South Side was the power of the churches there. At this point in his life, Obama did not have strong religious beliefs. But in Chicago, seeing how much respect people in the neighborhoods he was supposed to help had for the churches and the ministers, Obama said, "I figured I better attend some services myself and see what it was all about." Jeremiah A. Wright, the minister of the Trinity United Church of Christ, became an important person in Obama's life.

Wright became a mentor, teacher, and guide to Obama as Obama worked to understand the power of Christianity in the lives of black Americans. And he supported Obama as the young man developed from a questioner of religion to a practicing Christian. Later, when he campaigned for the Senate, Obama would never fail to carry his Bible. He would place it right beside him, in the small compartment in the passenger side door of the SUV, so he could refer to it often. "It's a great book and contains a lot of wisdom," he said simply. He was drawn to Christianity because its lessons of helping others and of selflessness reinforced his own beliefs about what is important in life.

At first, Obama had dreams of bringing the leaders of the Chicago churches together to work to make people's lives better. And this was the first hard lesson that Obama learned in Chicago: most of these ministers weren't willing to cooperate with each other. "It wasn't until I came to Chicago and started organizing that all this stuff that was in my head sort of was tested against the reality," Obama said. "And in some cases, it didn't always work out."

Wright counseled the young Obama that his

dream of bringing the Chicago pastors together was not realistic:

> He came up with this dream of organizing the churches of Chicago. . . . I said to him, "Oh, that sounds good, Barack, real good. But you don't know Chicago, do you?" Barack said to me, "You are a minister. Why are you sounding so skeptical?". . . And I said, "Man, these preachers in Chicago. You are not going to organize us. That's not going to happen." He had this really refreshing dream and I was like, "Barack, no, no, no. Not going to happen."

But Obama found other ways to make a difference in Chicago. A large part of community organizing is listening. The organizer has to hear and understand the fears and the hopes and the lives of the people he or she hopes to bring together. Working out of a small office in a church, Obama did twenty to thirty interviews each week, hearing what people had to say and slowly gaining their trust. "I'm here to do serious work," he told them.

Obama's first big project was to help the people of a housing project called Altgeld Gardens. About two thousand people, nearly all of them black, lived in this apartment near a huge garbage dump, a sewage plant, a paint factory, and the polluted Calumet River. Obama got groups together to demand that the Chicago Housing Authority, which was responsible for Altgeld Gardgens, repair toilets, windows, and the heating system.

Obama also helped to organize two meetings that drew attention to the asbestos problem in Altgeld. Asbestos is used for many purposes in buildings. But when asbestos fibers get old and break, tiny particles can drift into the air. If people breathe them, these particle can cause sickness, including cancer. The city government was pushed into hiring workers to seal off the asbestos in Altgeld so that it could not cause any harm.

Obama's time in Chicago helped shape who he became as a politician. Community organizing taught him that idealism must be combined with a practical understanding of what will work. Organizing also turned him into a careful listener to other people's concerns. He described the kind of work he did in Chicago as a powerful way to move America closer to its ideals of equality and justice for all:

In helping a group of housewives sit across the negotiating table with the mayor

of America's third largest city and hold their own, or a retired steelworker stand before a TV camera and give voice to the dreams he has for his grandchild's future, one discovers the most significant and satisfying contribution organizing can make.

In return, organizing teaches as nothing else does the beauty and strength of everyday people. Through the songs of the church and the talk on the stoops, through the hundreds of individual stories of coming up from the South and finding any job that would pay, of raising families on threadbare budgets, of losing some children to drugs and watching others earn degrees and land jobs their parents could never aspire to—it is through these stories . . . that organizers can shape a sense of community not only for others, but for themselves.

Harvard

We had the sense . . . that he genuinely cared what the conservatives had to say and what they thought and that he would listen to their ideas with an open mind.

—Brad Berenson, a Harvard Law School classmate

Before his work in Chicago, Barack Obama had not met with failure often. He had usually found at least a little success at whatever he tried, from pickup basketball to college classes to attracting young women.

At first, one of his biggest organizing projects—the campaign to get rid of asbestos in Altgeld Gardens—seemed to be a small victory for Obama. But then government officials told the people living at Altgeld that they had a choice between repairing the building's plumbing and leaky roof or cleaning up the poisonous asbestos—there was not enough money to do both. This left many wondering what all their hard work had accomplished. "Ain't nothing gonna change, Mr. Obama," one of the people at Altgeld complained. Obama grew increasingly frustrated.

At about the same time, Chicago's African-American community suffered a tragic setback. In November 1987, the city's first black mayor, Harold Washington, had a heart attack at his desk and died. Thousands attended his two-day wake in the lobby of City Hall. "Everywhere black people appeared dazed, stricken, uncertain of direction, frightened of the future," Obama wrote.

Bobby Titcomb, his friend from the Punahou Academy, visited Obama around this time. "I just can't get things done here without a law degree," Obama told Titcomb. "I've got to get a law degree to do anything against these guys because they've got their little loopholes and this and that. A law degree—that's the only way to work against these guys." Mayor Washington, as Obama knew, had been a lawyer. Obama had watched closely as Washington used his power to help the city's minority communities. Washington could do more for Chicago's poor blacks than Obama could in countless days and nights of community meetings.

Obama arrived at Harvard Law School at twenty-seven, several years older than most of his classmates. He was now working harder at his studies than ever before, and his grades reflected his effort.

As he had in New York and Chicago, Obama spent a vast amount of time by himself at Harvard. In his first year, he would carve out a spot for himself in the library and burrow in for several hours of intense study every day.

Obama again made friendships with the small number of black students on campus. But he also reached out and found several close white friends. He researched and wrote articles for a magazine, the *Harvard Civil Rights–Civil Liberties Law Review*. He was active in the anti-apartheid movement on campus and gave a speech at the annual dinner hosted by the Black Law Students Association.

Obama immediately made a mark at Harvard. He went to work for liberal professor Laurence Tribe and impressed him so much that Tribe would later call Obama his "most amazing research assistant." Later he added, "He's a guy I hope will be president someday."

Obama made long-lasting friendships at Harvard, one with a black woman named Cassandra Butts. The two met in the financial aid office the first week of classes. Obama's personal charm, interesting background, and unique point of view intrigued her.

"The experience that he had from his work as an organizer, the international experience that he had—he just saw the world in a different way than anyone I had met, to that point, and definitely anyone who was in law school with us," she explained. "And so that, you know, that just made him interesting. . . . He came to discussions with much more life experience than most of the students. I mean, we all had big ideas, but Barack had the experience."

Obama's different, more practical point of view was obvious during a large organized discussion among black students of Harvard's law, medical, and business schools. The meeting was to discuss a hot topic of the day among educated blacks: should they refer to themselves as "blacks" or "African Americans"? People argued heatedly for each side. But when Obama stood up to speak, he didn't take sides. He said the whole issue did not matter in the real world. As Butts remembered it, Obama told the crowd: "You know, whether we're called black or African Americans doesn't make a whole heck of a lot of difference to the lives of people who are working hard, you know, living day to day, in Chicago, in New York. That's not what's going to make a difference in their lives. It's how we use our education in these next three years to make their lives better."

Obama's most important experience at Harvard would be his time as a writer, editor and, finally, president of the *Harvard Law Review*, one of the most famous journals, or magazines, about the law in the whole country. His work on the *Review* gave Obama his first lesson in managing people who strongly disagreed with one another.

In 1990 about seventy-five students worked on the *Review*. Many were liberals. There were also small bands of conservatives. Each side was trying to push the *Review* in its own direction. Brad Berenson, a classmate of Obama, said that the fighting among the *Review* staff was "just ridiculously bitter."

At the last moment and at the urging of his friends, Obama decided to run for president of the *Review* in its 1990–1991 year. He was one of nineteen editors who tried to get the job. Finally, after almost a full day of voting by the law students who worked there, Obama was elected, the first African American to become president.

Berenson said that Obama won for various reasons, but race was not among them. Obama was a devoted liberal, but conservatives believed he would give their opinions a fair hearing. Berenson remembered that "Barack made no bones about the fact that he was a liberal, but you didn't get the sense that he was a partisan. . . . He was a more mature and more reasonable and more open-minded person. We had the sense . . . that he genuinely cared what the conservatives had to say and what they thought and that he would listen to their ideas with an open mind."

Obama, in fact, used some of his power to give conservatives important jobs on the *Review*. He insisted that each viewpoint deserved a fair hearing. The *Review* ran rather peacefully under his leadership. "He made people feel generally included and valued and he got everybody in harness, working toward a common goal," said Berenson.

Some people complained that Obama did not give more jobs on the review to African Americans. His friend Cassandra Butts said that Obama was fixed on making the best choices based on talent, dedication, and personality. Obama, for his part, said that "I had to manage a *Law Review* with seventy students who all want their own positions and who all want their advancement. And I had to make decisions about promoting diversity but also ensuring that people feel that I am being fair."

As his time at Harvard drew to an end, Obama began setting his sights on the mission that he had been training for—politics back in Chicago. "He wanted to be mayor of Chicago, and that was all he talked about," Butts said. "He never talked about the U.S. Senate; he never talked about being governor. He only talked about being mayor, because he felt that is really where you have an impact. That's where you could really make a difference in the lives of those people he had spent those years organizing. He could have gone on to great acclaim, but those people still were his mission."

7 Sweet Home Chicago

Barack was like, "Well, I wanna be a politician. You know, maybe I can be president of the United States." And I said, "Yeah, yeah, okay, come over and meet my Aunt Gracie—and don't tell anybody that!"

—Craig Robinson, Barack Obama's brother-in-law

Barack Obama seemed to know almost immediately upon meeting an African-American lawyer named Michelle Robinson that she was his choice for a wife; the young Miss Robinson was far less sure about her future husband. And that in itself says much about the two people: Barack is the romantic dreamer; Michelle is more realistic. Once he met her, he was swept off his feet; she took some convincing.

Obama and Robinson met after Obama's first year at Harvard Law, in 1988, when he had a summer job in a Chicago law firm. Robinson, a young lawyer there, was assigned to be his mentor. At first, Robinson was doubtful about Obama because he had been talked up by so many others in the company. Secretaries gossiped about how handsome he was. Lawyers marveled at his magnificent first-year performance at Harvard. Others said that a memo by Obama was brilliant. "He sounded too good to be true," Michelle remembered. "I figured he was one of these smooth brothers who could talk straight and impress people. So we had lunch, and he had this bad sport jacket and a cigarette dangling from his mouth and I thought, 'Oh, here you go. Here's this good-looking, smooth-talking guy. I've been down this road before.' Later I was just shocked to find out that he really could communicate with people and he had some depth to him."

Obama, on the other hand, was immediately taken with Michelle. But at first she would not go out with him. She thought it wouldn't be right to date an employee she was assigned to train. Michelle tried to set up Obama with a friend, but he showed no interest in anyone but her. Eventually, she agreed to a date, and, over chocolate ice cream at a Baskin-Robbins shop, he won her affection. When Obama returned to Harvard in the fall, the two kept up their relationship.

During his late twenties, Obama also began considering the value of marriage and family. He thought about his father's difficult family life and longed for something different for himself.

Michelle Obama grew up in the South Shore neighborhood of Chicago's South Side. The Robinsons lived in a small apartment on the top floor of a bungalow. Michelle's father, Frasier Robinson, worked at the city's water filtration plant. Her mother, Marian, did not work outside the home until Michelle reached high school, when she took a job in a bank. Michelle has one sibling, a brother, Craig, sixteen months older than she. A talented basketball player, he is the head coach at Brown University.

Michelle and Craig's father suffered from an illness that family members believe was multiple sclerosis. But he was devoted to setting a good example as a father and providing for his family. He rarely missed work or time with his children, even as his illness got worse. "We always felt like we couldn't let Dad down because he worked so hard for us," Craig Robinson said. "My sister and I, if one of us ever got in trouble with my father, we'd both be crying. We'd both be like, 'Oh, my god, Dad's upset. How could we do this to him?'"

Unusually tall at five feet eleven inches, Michelle was a good athlete, holding her own on the basketball court with her brother and his friends. But to avoid comparisons with her brother, she decided not to play organized sports. Instead, she played the piano, wrote short stories in her spiral notebook, became student council treasurer, and excelled in school. She skipped the second grade and usually made the honor roll in high school. Then she went on to Princeton University.

At Princeton, for the first time in her life, Michelle was in a setting that was nearly all white. And even though she was popular and quickly found a handful of good friends, she admitted that she felt isolated as one of the few black women on the campus. "I sometimes feel like a visitor on campus, as if I really don't belong," she wrote at the time. But she did well in college and graduated with honors.

After Princeton, she took a high-paying job at the law firm where she would meet her future husband. Yet a few years later, after marrying Obama, Michelle found herself moving into jobs where she could focus on helping others. She worked for Mayor Richard M. Daley and later created a program that helped young people find jobs in public service.

Michelle's mother, Marian Robinson, was fond of Obama but was worried that his biracial background might create difficulties for the couple, or that their marriage might not be easily accepted by others. Michelle's brother, Craig, on the other hand, was impressed by Obama's performance on the basketball court. Obama was not as good an athlete as Craig. But he was eager to step on the court with the former college star. "Barack's game is just like his personality—he's confident, not afraid to shoot the ball when he's open. See, that says a lot about a guy," Craig said. "A lot of guys wanna just be out there to say they were out there. But he wants to be out there and be a part of the game. He wants to try and win and he wants to try and contribute."

This self-confidence became a part of Obama's character early in life. His grandfather would tell Obama that the greatest lesson he could learn from his absent father was that confidence is the secret to success.

Even though Craig was impressed by Obama's basketball skills, he was startled at a holiday gathering when Obama told him that he might try a new career after law school: politics. "Barack was like, 'Well, I wanna be a politician. You know, maybe I can be president of the United States,'" Craig remembered. "And I said, 'Yeah, yeah, okay, come over and meet my Aunt Gracie—and don't tell anybody that!' "

Michelle was encouraging about Obama's hopes. "I told him, 'If that's what you really want to do, I think you'd be great at it,'" she said. "'You are everything people say they want in their public officials.'" But while she thought he had great talent, she also thought he was something of a dreamer. He might be a star in the world of politics one day, but that was of little interest to her. Even more than Obama's intelligence and personal charm, what sealed Michelle's love for him was his sense of decency and compassion. She was touched by his treatment of one of her uncles who had a drinking problem. Obama could easily have dismissed the man. Instead, "Barack treated him with respect and dignity, like an equal," Michelle said.

Michelle and Obama married after a four-year courtship. They settled in Chicago's Hyde Park neighborhood on the city's South Side. Hyde Park is one of a few neighborhoods in Chicago where both blacks and whites live in large numbers.

When Obama returned to Chicago from Harvard, he first took a job in charge of a campaign to sign up people to vote, especially black people with low incomes. Illinois Project Vote registered nearly 150,000 new voters for the 1992 presidential election. But while running Project Vote by day, Obama was writing his first book, *Dreams from My Father*, at night, leaving Michelle feeling rather lonely. This would happen often in their life together: Obama would burden himself with too much work, leaving little time for his family. "There are times when I want to do everything and be everything," he admitted. "I want to have time to read and swim with the kids and not disappoint my voters and do a really careful job on each and every thing that I do. And that can sometimes get me into trouble. . . . I mean, I was trying to organize Project Vote at the same time as I was writing a book, and there are only so many hours in a day."

Michelle has also said that Obama's urge to win sometimes makes him brag too much after winning family games, such as Scrabble or Monopoly. She calls her husband the "Fact Guy." "He seems to have a fact about everything," she claimed. "He can argue and debate about anything. It doesn't matter if he agrees with you, he can still argue with you. Sometimes, he's even right."

After Project Vote was over, Obama chose a job at the law firm of Miner, Barnhill & Galland, whose attorneys work mainly on civil rights and discrimination cases. They tried to fix injustice through the courts. Over the nine years that Obama worked in law in Illinois, he never handled a trial. Mostly he worked in teams of lawyers who wrote documents and contracts.

Judson Miner, one of the partners at the law firm, was also part of the reason Obama chose Miner, Barnhill & Galland. Miner had worked for Mayor Harold Washington and knew many people in Chicago politics. Obama had seen how much Washington had accomplished as mayor—more than Obama thought he could accomplish working only as a lawyer. "The courts are generally very slow," he said. "So it was at this point that I started thinking more seriously about political office."

8 Politics

People are hungry for community; they miss it.
They are hungry for change.

—Barack Obama

When a chance to run for public office came in 1995, Obama seized it. A state senator, Alice Palmer, had decided to leave the Illinois General Assembly and run for Congress. (The state senate is part of the General Assembly, whose members, like Palmer, vote on state laws for Illinois. Illinois, like all other states, also chooses senators who go to Congress in Washington, D.C., to vote on laws for the entire country.) Obama decided to run in an election for Palmer's former seat in the state senate. Palmer supported Obama as her replacement.

But that is only where the story begins.

Obama says that Palmer agreed not to compete with him for the state senate, whether or not she won her election to Congress. But when it looked like Palmer would lose, her supporters met with Obama. They asked him if he would step aside if Palmer didn't win. Then she could run again for the state senate, but Obama would not be able to run for anything.

Obama thought that Palmer was going back on her agreement. He told Palmer's people that he would not quit the race.

Palmer did, indeed, lose the election to Congress and then quickly decided to run for her old seat. Suddenly, Obama was facing a much tougher race. But he had one card up his sleeve. He discovered that there was a problem with the petitions people had signed so that Palmer could run in the election. Palmer withdrew from the race and Obama easily won the fall election. Now he was a state senator.

A newspaper, the *Chicago Reader*, published a long article on Obama, including many of Obama's own words about his views on race and politics. This was the first time he was able to tell Chicago as a whole what he believed. The ideas he laid out in this article are very much the same as those he supports today: people must learn to work together to build healthy communities. As Obama put it:

> People are hungry for community; they
> miss it. They are hungry for change. . . .
> Now we have to take . . . these same values
> that are encouraged within our families—of
> looking out for one another, of sharing, of
> sacrificing for each other—and apply them
> to a larger society. Let's talk about creating a
> society, not just individual families, based on
> these values.

At Harvard, Obama's practice of patiently listening
to all sides made him popular and eased conflict
with people who worked on the *Law Review*. But at
first he was not popular with everyone in the
General Assembly in Springfield, Illinois. In fact,
the man who soon became Obama's chief political
adviser admitted that he did not care for Obama at
their first meeting. Dan Shomon was a reporter who
had become an aide to Democrats in the state capi-
tal. Obama noticed that Shomon worked hard for
the senator in the office next door. So he asked to
have Shomon assigned to him, as well.

Shomon's first reaction was: "He wants to change
the world and that is great, but I don't really like the
guy that much." Still, Shomon agreed to meet with
Obama, and when Obama took Shomon out for

dinner, the two wound up getting along well. So Shomon went to work for Obama.

Shomon told Obama that, because he would be voting on issues that affected people living outside Chicago, he should travel around the state so that he would understand more about Illinois. Obama responded without hesitation: "Let's do it." (In Obama's second book, he says the idea of this first trip was actually his.)

On this trip and later ones, both Shomon and Obama wanted to see how voters outside of Chicago would react to Obama as an African-American politician. Southern Illinois, in particular, has a long history of racial intolerance. At Illinois's southern tip, the small town of Cairo has a past that includes the lynching of black men in the early 1900s and a race riot in 1967. While traveling in a small town on a later trip, Obama and Shomon were pulled over by a police officer when they accidentally turned the wrong direction down a one-way street. When Shomon told the officer that Obama was a state senator, the man "looked flabbergasted," Shomon said. "He's not a state senator from these parts!" the officer told Shomon.

Still, in most places, Obama discovered that everyday people reacted warmly to him. "It was just a great trip because it really did open Barack's eyes," Shomon said. "He thinks these people are really cool, and they could relate to him—although, you know, they couldn't pronounce his name."

These mostly white, middle-class, down-to-earth midwestern people reminded Obama of his grandparents and he felt completely comfortable in their midst. "I understand these folks," Obama said. "I grew up with these people."

The Legislator

I always found him to be a true gentleman in all the . . . dealings that I had with him.

— Joe Birkett, Republican county prosecutor

No one rolled out a red carpet for Obama when he arrived in Springfield, Illinois, in January 1997. "It wasn't like Barack took Springfield by storm," Dan Shomon said. "The first few years he was thought of as intelligent, thoughtful, bright. But he certainly wasn't considered to be a major player." Some people involved in Springfield politics thought of Obama as a snob. "Barack is a very intelligent man," the publisher of a newsletter said. "He hasn't had a lot of success here [in Springfield], and it could be because he places himself above everybody. He likes people to know he went to Harvard."

Even so, Obama learned to get along in Springfield. He started to play golf. He made close friends with a number of fellow lawmakers. He joined a weekly poker game that included other senators. As he did when playing board games at home, Obama took the game seriously and tried hard to win.

One of Obama's most important relationships was with Emil Jones Jr., an African American who had started as a Chicago sewer inspector and become a state lawmaker. Obama had actually met Jones while he was still a community organizer. He had organized a neighborhood meeting near Jones's home, and when the meeting turned into a small march, Jones stepped outside to see what was going on. Obama and Jones would grow so close that Jones would talk about the fatherless Obama as a son. "Emil is driven by a sense that the African-American community has not been given its fair share and he is trying to make up for that—and I respect that mission," Obama said. Jones puts his fondness for Obama in more personal terms. "I am blessed to be his godfather and he feels like a son to me," Jones said.

In his first term, Obama managed to pass a decent number of laws. He worked closely with white Democrats and even conservatives to get laws made. After working harmoniously with conservatives on the *Harvard Law Review*, Obama was not the least bit uncomfortable taking the concerns of Illinois conservatives into account. His polite manner was key to his success. "I always found him to be a true gentleman in all the . . . dealings that I had with him," said Joe Birkett, a Republican.

"The most important thing that you do in Springfield is you bring all sides of an issue to the table and you make them feel they are being listened to," said Obama. This reasonable tone and honest attention to Republican concerns made Obama an important person in Illinois politics. "Members of both parties listened closely to him," said a Republican senator who often worked with Obama.

But as Obama's first term in the state senate drew to an end, he made his first major political mistake.

Obama had returned to Chicago from Harvard Law with an eye on the mayor's office. But by 2000, Obama didn't think he or anyone had much of a chance of defeating the current mayor, Richard M. Daley. So Obama looked at Congress instead. He decided to run against Bobby Rush in the 2000 Democratic primary election for a chance at winning a seat in the House of Representatives. Whichever of the two Democrats won the primary would go on to face a Republican in the general election later.

But Rush was an African American admired by many black voters, who admired his past in the civil rights movement of the 1960s and his work for Harold Washington, the first black mayor of Chicago. Some voters wondered what Obama was doing when he decided to challenge Rush. Obama had not been brought up in a traditional African-American home, and people questioned if he really understood or even cared about the lives of African Americans.

For his part, Obama insists the complaint that he is "not black enough" is just a lie drummed up by politicians who don't agree with him. "It's never been an issue among regular folks on the street," he said. "You know, it's never an issue with the bus drivers or the teachers or the guys on the street corner who I'm talking to."

Five months before the primary election, Bobby Rush's twenty-nine-year-old son was killed. The public now had so much sympathy for Rush that it looked impossible for Obama to win many votes against him. And then came another problem.

In December 1999 Obama and Michelle and their daughter, Malia, now eighteen months old, went to visit Obama's grandmother in Honolulu. Obama had looked forward all year to spending a couple of weeks where he grew up. But in 1999 an important gun-control law came up for a vote while Obama was gone. Obama supported the bill and would have voted for it, but he couldn't vote from Hawaii.

Shomon, his aide, got on the phone with Obama and told his boss that he ought to consider returning to Illinois. Obama, however, had been spending a lot of time away from Michelle and their young daughter. Michelle did not want him to leave the family vacation early for the sake of work. And Malia had come down with a bad cold. Obama was torn between his duty as senator and his duty as a father and husband. In the end, he chose to remain in Hawaii.

The gun-control bill did not pass. The governor of Illinois was angry at Obama, and Obama was criticized in the *Chicago Tribune*, an important newspaper.

"I cannot sacrifice the health or well-being of my daughter for politics," Obama told reporters. But after that, Obama knew that he was probably not going to win against Bobby Rush. "Less than halfway into the campaign, I knew in my bones that I was going to lose," he wrote.

Obama was right. He lost the election.

◆ ◆ ◆

Obama stood outside a polling place on the day of the primary against Bobby Rush. One after another, voters told him that they liked him and thought he had a bright future, but they couldn't vote for him. The reason was summed up by one elderly woman who explained to Obama, "Bobby just ain't done nothin' wrong."

It became clear to Obama that he had been thinking of himself and his career rather than what the voters needed or wanted. When Obama returned to Springfield, his coworkers and friends saw that he was a changed man. He had not just lost to Rush, but in Obama's own words, he had been "spanked."

Yet instead of sulking, Obama got back to work. And instead of holding grudges against those who had not supported him in the election, Obama worked to improve relations with them.

Obama also spent some time wondering if he wanted to keep working in politics. In 2001 his second child, Sasha, was born. With two children, Michelle longed to have a husband with more time to spend at home. And the campaign had been expensive. "I was broke," Obama recalled. "And not only that, but my wife was mad at me because we had a baby and I had made this run for Congress. . . . It wasn't a high point in my life."

This was perhaps the first time that Obama began to consider the importance of money. He had always been generous with his friends and the people who worked for him. But he didn't care much about being wealthy or buying expensive things for himself or his family. He hated buying new clothes, telling Michelle to pick out a couple of new shirts and ties for him at Christmas. His socks were worn in the heels, and his winter coat was ten years old.

Now Obama wondered about taking a job outside of politics, where he might make more money. But he could not see himself making such a move. In 2002, Obama began to think about the U.S. Senate race in 2004. Yet nearly everyone close to Obama gave him the same advice: don't run.

His wife, Michelle, and his top aide and good friend, Shomon, both said so. Shomon was worried about Obama's family. "I told Barack, 'I don't think you should run,'" Shomon remembered. "I said I thought it was a bad idea because of Michelle and the kids. Barack feels tremendous guilt. He has a conscience. I thought he would wish he hadn't done it afterward. But he just looked at me and said, 'I'm running anyway.'"

10 The Candidate

*What I want to do is roll the dice and
put everything we have into this thing.*

—Barack Obama

Obama had serious conversations with his fellow
Illinois lawmakers about his idea of running for
the Senate. Several promised to support him. But
there was one other person whose agreement was
necessary—Michelle.

Michelle knew that her husband's political career
was extremely important to him. But when she
heard his Senate idea, she began to wonder if this
optimistic dreamer was going off the deep end. After
Obama's crushing loss to Bobby Rush, she worried
that her husband was about to try the impossible.
And she worried about money. Another political
race could keep the family in debt.

"The big issue around the Senate for me was, how

on earth can we afford it?" Michelle said. "How are we going to get by? . . . And we're trying to save for college for the girls. . . . My thing is, is this just another gamble? . . . And he said, 'Well, then, I'm going to write a book, a good book.' And I'm thinking . . . 'Just write a book, yeah, that's right. Yep, yep, yep. And you'll climb the beanstalk and come back down with the golden egg, Jack.'"

But Obama was confident. He explained, "What I told Michelle is that politics has been a huge strain on you, but I really think there is a strong possibility that I can win this race. . . . I said to her that if you are willing to go with me on this ride and if it doesn't work out, then I will step out of politics. . . . I think that Michelle felt as if I was sincere. I think she had come to realize that I would leave politics if she asked me to."

Michelle said, "Whatever. We'll figure it out. . . . Go ahead." Then she laughed and told him hopefully, "And maybe you'll lose."

Obama went back to Shomon and told him he was going to run. "So I told Dan that I had this conversation with Michelle and she had given me the green light and that what I want to do is roll the dice and put everything we have into this thing."

Obama knew he would need to raise a lot of money. So he invited a group of African Americans who might help to the house of a friend, Marty Nesbitt. "Barack says he wants to run for the U.S. Senate," Nesbitt recalled. "*Blahhh!* I mean, I literally fell off the couch. And we all started laughing—and he said, 'No, really, I am gonna run for the U.S. Senate.'" Obama proceeded to make a logical argument that he could win. "He convinced us in the room that day that he could pull it off," Nesbitt said. Obama also told them the hard truth: he was going to need not hundreds of thousands but millions of dollars to pull off a victory.

Nesbitt said that Obama's confidence, clear vision, and attention to detail convinced them that it was doable. It certainly wasn't a sure win, but it was doable.

Obama realized that he needed more people with political talent working for him. He turned to a political consultant, David Axelrod. A couple of years earlier, Axelrod and his wife, Susan, had thrown a quick fund-raiser for Obama at their downtown Chicago condominium. About twenty people showed up. "We were pulling in people from the pool, urging them, 'Hey, come meet your new state senator,'" Axelrod said.

Axelrod told the hopeful Obama that he thought Obama was a "terrific talent" and said, "I consider you my friend," but he probably couldn't win a race for the Senate. Axelrod thought that Obama should wait until the mayor of Chicago retired and try for that job.

That disappointed Obama, but it did not stop him—he still thought the Senate was a good possibility. But he soon encountered an even bigger problem. Carol Moseley Braun, who had been an Illinois senator from 1993 to 1999 and made history as the first African-American woman to serve in the Senate, announced that she might run for the Senate again. If she were to run, Obama said, he would have to stay out of the race.

Obama talked to his pastor and friend, the Reverend Jeremiah A. Wright. He slumped onto the sofa in the pastor's second-floor office at Trinity United Church of Christ and told Wright that the Senate idea was frustrating him because Moseley Braun would not make up her mind whether she was in or out. And not only that, but other politicians had begun to suggest that they might run as well. "My name should be out there," Obama told his pastor. "But Carol Moseley Braun won't say what she's going to do, and I'm not gonna run against a black woman. If she's gonna run, then I'm out. Until she says yes or no, I can't say anything."

A few months later, Obama took his yearly Christmas trip to Hawaii. The forty-one-year-old Illinois state senator was worried that all his hard work was coming to nothing. The frustrating years trying to organize programs that would help the poor on Chicago's South Side, the years working in the Illinois General Assembly, the days and nights away from his wife and two precious daughters to travel the campaign trail—what had this sacrifice done for him and for the world? Suddenly Obama's grand idea of winning an election to the Senate looked like a dream.

For the first time, Obama was deeply frightened. He was terrified that the final tale of Barack Obama's political career would be this: another talented black man with big dreams somehow flamed out and disappeared from public life. Most frightening of all, this story was too much like the story of his father, who had not achieved his potential in life.

But then Obama looked at his two young girls splashing in the ocean with Michelle. They looked playful and happy. Obama thought, well, perhaps he was not meant to be a senator or a mayor. "I didn't grow up thinking that I wanted to be a politician,"

Obama recalled. "If this doesn't work out I am fine with it. . . . I had to remind myself that it was not all about me and my personal ambitions."

But just as Obama was thinking that his grand political career might never happen, he received a phone call. Moseley Braun had decided not to run for the Senate. Obama knew exactly what he needed to do—and fast. He flipped his cell phone open and dialed David Axelrod.

11 The Consultant

*I thought that if I could help Barack Obama
get to Washington, then I would have
accomplished something great in my life.*

—David Axelrod, political consultant

Without David Axelrod working for him, Obama
might not have won the Democratic Party primary
in his race for the Senate. And even if Obama had
still managed to win without Axelrod, he wouldn't
have done it in such an astonishing fashion—in a
way that made him a national star even before he
hit Washington. Obama had the talent for success.
But Axelrod was the coach who took that talent and
polished it, and then made sure Obama was known
to Illinois voters. Obama relied heavily on Axelrod
during the 2003–2004 campaign—and after that
too. If Obama was talking on his cell phone, which
he seemed to be doing at every spare moment, he
was likely to be talking with "Ax."

A native of New York City, Axelrod is a tall man who was then nearly fifty years old. He has a thick salt-and-pepper mustache, thinning hair, a slouch, and dark, droopy eyes that make him appear sad. He has a keen sense of humor, but he doesn't often smile at his own wit. Axelrod did his first political work at the age of nine, when he handed out leaflets for Robert Kennedy's campaign for Senate. "I just wanted to go out and do it and so I went over and volunteered—I was a weird kid," Axelrod said.

Axelrod is a former reporter for the *Chicago Tribune*. He came to the city to study at the University of Chicago and, just days after graduation, found himself at the paper. He worked his way up to writing stories about politics.

After leaving the newspaper in 1984, Axelrod became a political consultant, giving politicians advice on how to run their campaigns. He was hired to work on the Senate campaign of Paul Simon, whose devotion and honesty inspired him. Still in his twenties, Axelrod went from newspaper reporting to handling a major Senate campaign almost overnight.

No one has more talent than Axelrod at making television commercials that highlight the best points of a candidate. And, as a former *Tribune* reporter, he had connections to Chicago's media. He could call nearly any political reporter or newspaper editor in the Chicago region and get his calls returned. Axelrod throws a December holiday party each year. About half the guests work in media—newspapers, magazines, or television. The other half are politicians or those who work with them. Each serious candidate in the 2004 Senate contest wanted to hire Axelrod.

The candidate who seemed most likely to do that was Blair Hull. Hull was a former gambler from Las Vegas who had become extremely wealthy in the stock market. He had promised to spend tens of millions of dollars on the Senate campaign—whatever it took to win a seat.

But after meeting with him, Axelrod didn't feel that Hull had the talent to win. And he was worried over rumors about problems in Hull's personal life. When Hull wouldn't say that the rumors were untrue, Axelrod looked elsewhere for a job.

In 2002, Barack Obama delivered what he believes to be his best speech ever—an address to a group of war protestors in which he flatly stated that he was against a U.S. invasion of Iraq. The beginning of the Iraq war was still months away. Many voters approved of President George W. Bush. Polls showed that most Americans would stand behind him if he decided that a war with Iraq was in the best interests of the country.

A supporter of Obama, Bettylu Saltzman, organized a rally against the war in Chicago and asked Obama to give a speech. Saltzman admired Obama and had been helpful to him when he ran for the state senate in Illinois. "When he speaks, it's like—it's like magic," she said.

Obama told Saltzman that he would think over her request. This was one of the biggest decisions of his campaign for Senate. Should he take a public stand against an Iraq war before it even started, when no one knew how it would end? He talked with Dan Shomon. Shomon warned Obama to be careful with his words. Whatever he said could have a strong effect on his political future.

Obama called Saltzman just a couple of days before the event and told her that he would speak. He then went home and wrote his speech in a single evening. Up to this point in Obama's career, he had rarely written anything down when he talked in public. He relied on his talent for creating a speech as he went along. But this time he took

Shomon's advice about the importance of each word to heart. "I knew that this was going to be an important statement on an important issue," Obama said. He didn't want people to make any mistakes about what he meant. "I wanted to strike exactly what I truly felt on this thing. The nice thing is, because I thought the politics of [the invasion] were bad, it was liberating—because I said exactly what I truly believed."

Obama began his speech by announcing that he was "someone who is not opposed to war in all circumstances." He said this more than once—"I don't oppose all wars"—between explaining the blunt reasons he offered against sending troops to Iraq. "What I am opposed to is a dumb war," he said. "What I am opposed to is a rash war. . . . A war based not on reason but on passion, not on principle but on politics."

Obama warned that no one could know how long a U.S. occupation of Iraq would last, how much it would cost, and what its consequences would be. He was certain that an invasion without strong support from other countries would only "fan the flames of the Middle East and encourage the worst, rather than the best, impulses of the Arab world" and would also make it easier for the terrorist group Al Qaeda to recruit new members.

Over time these predictions became reality. The Iraq war slid into chaos, killing several thousand Americans and tens of thousands of Iraqis. This speech had placed Obama firmly and publicly against the Iraq invasion before it happened. Most Americans would gradually come to agree with him as the war dragged on. The speech would also make Obama the only candidate in the 2004 Senate race and the only well-known Democrat in the 2008 presidential race to flatly oppose the war before it began. Obama said that this had been his best-written and most courageous speech and was his favorite:

> That's the speech I'm most proud of. It was a hard speech to give, you know, because I was about to announce for the United States Senate and the politics were hard to read then. . . . You didn't know whether this thing was gonna play out like the first Gulf War, and you know, suddenly everybody's coming back to cheering. . . . And it was just, well, a well-constructed speech. I like it.

With Moseley Braun out of the Senate race, Obama was free and clear to announce that he would definitely run. He did so on January 21, 2003, at a downtown Chicago hotel.

At the time, Axelrod was still thinking over his choices. He had once told Obama to pass on the Senate race and wait to run for Chicago mayor one day. But he was beginning to change his mind. In Obama, he saw raw talent, strong drive, and a decent opportunity at winning.

"My involvement was a leap of faith," Axelrod said. "Barack showed flashes of brilliance as a candidate during the early stages of the campaign, but there were times of absolute pure drudgery. . . . But I thought that if I could help Barack Obama get to Washington, then I would have accomplished something great in my life."

To make Obama a better candidate, Axelrod did two things. First, he urged Obama to think more in terms of people and their stories rather than making long, dull speeches about plans for how he would govern. And he stressed the importance of this advice to Obama's other close adviser, Michelle Obama. Obama listens to her advice more than anyone else's, even Axelrod's.

Axelrod told Obama to imagine the people he had met and would be meeting on the campaign trail, to try to bring their stories to life in his speeches. "It clicked in his head and he became a much better candidate over time," Axelrod said. "Once he realized that he was not taking orals at Harvard he became a better candidate."

12 The Race Factor

Barack is a black man!
—Michelle Obama

Obama approached his friend Emil Jones Jr., president of the Illinois senate, about supporting his race for the Senate of the United States. "You know, you have a lot of power," Obama told Jones. "You can make the next U.S. senator." Jones answered, "Wow, that sounds good! Got anybody in mind?" Obama said, "Yes—me."

In 2003 and 2004, Jones saw to it that Obama had many bills to shepherd through the senate and turn into laws. This got Obama a lot of attention in Illinois. With Jones's help, over the next two years, Obama sponsored nearly eight hundred bills. Besides being good for Obama's political career, many of these new laws were to help children, the elderly, and the poor. "This is the kind of politics that I want to practice," Obama said. "This is why I am in this thing."

Obama has always talked about wanting to change society for the better. The three men he admires most are Mahatma Gandhi, Abraham Lincoln, and Martin Luther King Jr.—"men who were able to bring about extraordinary changes," he said. In an interview, he explained that this longing to change things is why he chose to go into politics:

> When I was in college, I decided I wanted to be part of bringing about social change in this country, and some of that is based on the values my family gave me. Some of it is based on, I think, my status as an African American in this country. And some of it is informed by my having lived abroad and having family in underdeveloped countries where the contrast between rich and poor is so sharp that it is hard to ignore injustice. . . . I took a lot of inspiration from the civil rights movement and the way the movement brought ordinary people into extraordinary positions of leadership. It struck me that lasting change came from the bottom up and not from the top

down. I have been chasing this same goal my entire adult career, and that is creating an America that is fairer, more compassionate, and has greater understanding between its various peoples.

By early 2003, four other Democrats were preparing to run for the seat in the U.S. Senate that Obama wanted. In the primary, one Democrat would be chosen by voters to face a Republican in the general election. Dan Hynes seemed to have the best chance to win. He was the state comptroller, the official in charge of the budget, and his father had been powerful in Illinois politics. The other candidates included Blair Hull, who had millions of dollars of his own money to spend, and Gery Chico, who had once worked for the mayor of Chicago.

Obama's campaign in early 2003 was being run by Dan Shomon. Shomon, however, felt burned out and did not want to spend the next year running a Senate campaign. He told Obama that he needed to find another campaign manager by spring. This news infuriated Obama, who could not understand how Shomon could abandon him. "This Senate thing," Shomon tried to explain to Obama, "that's your thing, Barack—it's not mine. My life is going a different way." Obama, however, still felt betrayed. The close friendship between the two men was never quite the same.

As the spring wound down, Obama's team still needed a full-time manager. Axelrod was hunting for one. He wanted someone who would know how to elect a black candidate in an area that was mostly white, and he thought he'd found him in Jim Cauley. "Just come to Chicago and meet Barack and see if you see what I see," Axelrod said to Cauley over the phone. "If you don't see it, no sweat." So Cauley flew to Chicago and had lunch with Obama. He did not necessarily see what Axelrod saw in the candidate. "They were working out of two small rooms, and frankly," Cauley said, "it looked like a campaign for the state senate, not the U.S. Senate." But he respected the people who asked him to join Obama's campaign, and so he agreed to be campaign manager.

Cauley is slightly balding and barrel-chested, and his Kentucky accent is thick, his speech plainspoken and straightforward. Cauley did not claim to be a genius, and he knew what his role was: to help Obama raise money, hire and organize staff and volunteers, and then turn out Obama's voters on election day. "Somebody's got to keep the trains running on time and make sure the money is coming in—and that's me," Cauley said.

As he set out on the campaign trail, Obama was careful to pay attention to two groups whose votes he needed: African Americans and liberals. An important supporter was the Reverend Jesse Jackson Sr., the best-known black leader in the country. Jackson had been an adviser to Obama for several years. Michelle had been friends with Jackson's daughter, Jacqueline, while they grew up on Chicago's South Side. As a teenager, Michelle had even babysat Jackson's son, Jesse Jr.

Obama worked hard to win votes in the black community. But some people asked: Was Obama "black enough" to win many African-American votes? Obama has white family members. He went to schools that are mostly white. "Some . . . are whispering that 'Barack is not black enough,'" a writer commented in the *Chicago Sun-Times*. "He's of mixed race, he hangs out in Hyde Park, and is a darling of white progressives; he's not to be trusted."

Many black people are familiar with this issue: a suspicion that a black person who is successful or wealthy or who has friends and connections among white people is "trying to be white" and can't understand or doesn't care about the lives and problems of ordinary African Americans. Yet no one could deny that Obama campaigned hard in the black community. Nearly every Sunday morning he would give a speech in one of Chicago's black churches. Stepping before the congregation, Obama would use inspiring words and his background as a state senator to educate the audience about himself. By the end, he would usually win over most of the crowd.

Obama's message to black audiences was similar to his speeches to other Democratic groups—a theme of hope in the goodness of the human spirit. But to groups of African Americans he usually mentioned his Christian faith and his home church on Chicago's South Side. And Obama went one step further. He spoke of his own success being a step in the larger success of blacks across the country. To a nearly all-black audience at Mars Hill Baptist Church in Chicago, Obama declared: "I am not running a race-based campaign. I am rooted in the African-American community, but not limited by it. I am campaigning everywhere."

This statement connects with a desire of many black Americans to be fully accepted into society, not to be limited by skin color, to be given an equal chance. Obama was letting people know that a vote for him was a vote for freedom of all African Americans.

Obama's most convincing argument to African Americans was not his powerful speeches but what he had accomplished in the Illinois senate for black people. In Obama's words, "I have not just talked the talk, I have walked the walk." Before black crowds, Obama counted all the laws helping the black community that he had personally written and gotten passed. When people in black churches heard this, they would nod their heads approvingly.

Michelle defended her husband against suggestions that he was "not black enough." In a Chicago public television program about her husband, she practically jumped out of her seat when the interviewer mentioned that a political foe of Obama's had said that he was merely a tool for powerful white people. "Barack *is* a black man!" she said firmly. In an interview, she explained why her response was so emotional. She said that people of her race who achieve success in school and who do not conform to stereotypes of what blacks should be like can be excluded or shunned by people in their own communities. She met similar problems when she was growing up. Michelle said:

> It's like that growing up, you know. You talk a certain type of English and then you have to cover that up on your way to school so you don't get your butt kicked. You know, we grew up with that. My brother faced it, we all faced it. . . . And fortunately I came from a family on both sides that didn't believe in that. . . . And that's the frustration, I think, that I felt with that issue because it reminded me of just the kind of things that I had to deal with growing up.

13 The Small Screen

Don't you think it would be cool to be a senator?
—Blair Hull, Democratic candidate for the Senate

In summer and fall 2003, David Axelrod managed to get some stories into the media that mentioned Obama as a possible star in the making. This helped Obama raise three million dollars for his campaign. It was nothing compared with Blair Hull's tens of millions of dollars, but it would be enough to run two to three weeks of ads on television and show that Obama was a serious candidate. And Obama got the support of some powerful labor unions, which meant their members were likely to vote for him.

Obama's strongest competition came from Dan Hynes, an experienced politician, and Blair Hull, who had never run in an election before but had a lot of money to spend. While interviewing someone for a job on his campaign, Hull had been asked why he wanted to run for the Senate. He'd simply responded, "Don't you think it would be cool to be a senator?" The job seeker was shocked that Hull didn't have any better reason and decided not to work for him.

Hull's campaign had shelled out hundreds of thousands of dollars to run television commercials and internet ads. Hull billboards appeared, it seemed, in every corner of the state. He paid supporters fifty dollars a day to act as volunteers and cheer for his speeches. But Hull was not a good speaker. He would trip over his lines and always seemed to be reading from a script. When it came out that Hull's second wife had accused him of threatening her and that he had abused drugs and alcohol, his campaign started to fall apart.

Meanwhile, Obama's campaign had been following a simple strategy: hold on to your money and postpone TV advertising until the final weeks, when voters finally are paying attention—and then blast the airwaves with as much force as you can. This was not as easy as it seemed. Just a month from the election, Obama was still unknown to most blacks and most Democrats in general. Some supporters began advising Obama to start running TV ads immediately. "Barack was concerned that we needed to be out there," Axelrod said. But Obama finally chose to follow the original plan and keep waiting.

The primary election drew closer, and Hull and Hynes spent much of their time attacking each other. Obama laughed and said, "I'm just trying to keep my head down while they fling arrows at each other."

As the race went on, it seemed that Hull's personal problems were wrecking his chances and that Hynes had nothing particularly special to offer to voters. "I knew Dan Hynes was not going to win that race," an Illinois Democrat said. "I've played basketball with both him and Obama—and Hynes played soft."

Obama's stump speech was the main focus of his campaign and the way he introduced himself to voters. A stump speech is the talk that a candidate gives over and over, to one group after another, changing the words slightly to reach different crowds but hitting the same ideas each time. Obama never wrote his speech down, but created it fresh each time he spoke. He would usually open with the same joke about his name by saying that people invariably call him something else—"Yo mama" or "Alabama." This line always drew a laugh. But

Obama delivered it so often that, after a while, he had to remind himself to smile in response. Then he would use his name as a way to introduce himself. ("My father was from Kenya, in Africa, which is where I got my name. *Barack* means 'blessed by God' in Swahili. My mother was from Kansas, which is where I got my accent from.") Then Obama would launch into the speech, telling people about the difference he saw between his own vision and the direction that Republican leaders were taking the country.

Obama would make slight changes to the familiar words as he spoke, depending on feedback from each particular audience. "My general attitude is practice, practice, practice," Obama said. "I was just getting more experienced and seeing what is working and what isn't, when I am going too long and when it is going flat. Besides campaigning, I have always said that one of the best places for me to learn public speaking was actually teaching—standing in a room full of thirty or forty kids and keeping them engaged, interested, and challenged. I also think that David [Axelrod] was always very helpful in identifying what worked and what didn't in my speeches."

Obama's ability to connect with a black audience

Obama (front row, fourth from right) gathers with his classmates for their ninth-grade class picture at Punahou Academy.
(*Courtesy of Punahou School*)

Obama and the members of the Ka Wai Ola ("Living Water") Club meet on the steps of Punahou Academy in 1976.
(*Courtesy of Punahou School*)

Obama makes a lay-up for the Punahou team, but after arguing with his coach about the lack of playing time, Obama spent most games warming the bench. *(Courtesy of Punahou School)*

"Barry" Obama smiles for his senior class portrait at Punahou Academy in Honolulu in 1979.
(Courtesy of Punahou School)

The media flocks to interview Barack Obama as he arrives at his office in the Dirksen Senate Office Building for the first time.
(Photo by Scott J. Ferrell/Congressional Quarterly/Getty Images)

Delegates show their support for Obama as he delivers the keynote address at the Democratic National Convention on July 27, 2004. *(Photo by ROBYN BECK/AFP/Getty Images)*

Family time! Barack Obama wraps his arms around his wife, Michelle, and their daughters, Malia (right) and Sasha, in November 2004. *(Courtesy of Reuters)*

Senator Obama speaks before the Senate Foreign Relations Committee on January 18, 2005, in Washington, D.C. *(Photo by Matthew Cavanaugh/Getty Images)*

In Nairobi, Kenya, Gregory Ochieng holds a portrait of Barack Obama high above his head. Ochieng gave the painting to Obama when he visited Nairobi in August 2006. "He is my tribesman," he said. *(Courtesy of David Mendell)*

Barack Obama, with his half sister, Auma Obama, and his paternal grandmother, Sarah Hussein Obama, answers media questions on his father's farming compound in western Kenya in August 2006. (Courtesy of David Mendell)

Democratic presidential candidates Hillary Clinton and Barack Obama stand side by side at the CNN/YouTube Democratic presidential candidate debate in July 2007. (Photo by STAN HONDA/AFP/Getty Images)

Presidential hopeful Barack Obama takes his wife, Michelle, and daughters, Malia (second from left) and Sasha, on the campaign trail.
(Photo by Scott Olson/Getty Images)

Obama and famous supporter Oprah Winfrey embrace at a campaign event in Iowa in December 2007. (Photo by Scott Olson/ Getty Images)

PROGRESS

grew tremendously during the Senate race. And his message remained the same: Americans are linked by a common bond of humanity, and the country's government must reflect that. "I am my brother's keeper! I am my sister's keeper!" he proclaimed, his rich voice booming.

Obama's primary campaign faced only one serious problem. Paul Simon, a former senator from Illinois who had once run for president, planned to support Obama. Sadly, he died a week before he made the announcement. Simon was loved by Democrats throughout the state. Axelrod had planned to shoot a television commercial with Simon's personal support of Obama. That would have sent a message that Obama was like Simon: liberal, honest, and definitely his own man.

Instead, Axelrod created an ad that showed Simon's adult daughter comparing Obama with her father. Sheila Simon declared that Obama was the person who would best carry on her father's work. The ad turned out to be a huge success, showing Obama in a positive way to voters who had most likely never heard of him.

In those final three weeks, Obama's campaign ran several more of Axelrod's television ads. The first introduced Obama to voters, talking about his time at Harvard and his community organizing experience. The theme was "Yes, we can." "Now they say we can't change Washington," Obama said in an earnest voice. "I'm Barack Obama and I am running for the United States Senate to say, 'Yes, we can.'"

When Obama first saw the "Yes, we can" commercials, he was not impressed. He thought the idea was not serious enough and was something of a cliché. But Axelrod stood fast behind the ads and their message. So Obama went to his most trusted adviser—Michelle—and asked what she thought. She told him that the ads were a good idea and that he should use them. Obama accepted her judgment.

Earlier in his career, he might have kept arguing with Axelrod. "Barack is extremely intelligent, and one of the pitfalls of extreme intelligence is, you are so accustomed to being right that you believe you are always right," Axelrod observed. But after the Bobby Rush disaster, Obama discovered that, when it came to politics, there were people who could offer wisdom beyond his. It was probably smart to follow the advice of someone like Axelrod, especially if his wife agreed with it.

Other commercials displayed Obama's experience in the state senate and his ability to work hand in hand with Republicans. There was an image of

Obama walking next to a farmer, with silos and green fields in the background. Obama stood in front of a small-town courthouse and asked: "What if folks in office spent their time attacking problems instead of each other?" Perhaps the most powerful ad that Axelrod created showed Obama's connections to Paul Simon and Harold Washington, the former mayor of Chicago.

Obama put a lot of hard work into his speeches. But it was these television ads that pushed him over the top in the final three weeks of the race. Even the spokesman for the Hull campaign exclaimed, "Obama is on fire!"

Just a month before, Obama had been a little-known state senator. Seventy-two hours from the biggest election in his career, perhaps the biggest single moment of his life to date, all the polls showed that he had jumped from third place to first of all the Democratic candidates.

14 A Victory

Truthfully, it feels like a movement.
I think for people of our generation,
we haven't been a part of something like this before.
—An Obama voter

David Axelrod's strategy of holding onto the campaign's money and spending it on TV ads only at the end proved to be genius. Obama was soaring in the polls. This was the very beginning of the Obama phenomenon that would sweep through Illinois and then spread across the country, carrying him into the U.S. Senate and finally into the 2008 presidential race.

When Obama was in public places now, he was recognized. "Hey, that's Barack Obama," a black man whispered to a friend with a beaming smile on his face as Obama marched through a convention center in Chicago. Obama's campaign also attracted a flock of volunteers who believed in him. Many of them were college students who had heard of Obama from friends or family or had seen him speak. "We have all these save-the-world types showing up at the door," campaign manager Cauley mused one day. "Sometimes, I don't know what to do with them all."

The other candidates in the Democratic primary brainstormed about how to stop Obama in those final weeks, but they came up with nothing. Obama's campaign, however, did make a mistake. His staff mailed a flyer that seemed to be intended to convince voters to choose Obama, but the state government paid for it. It was mailed just a few days before a deadline when all such mailings were supposed to stop. The law putting a limit on these kinds of mailings was written by Obama himself.

The *Chicago Tribune* broke the story. The Obama campaign had done nothing illegal, but did not seem to be following the spirit of the law that Obama had worked to get passed. The *Tribune* story began like this: "The Democratic U.S. Senate candidate [Obama] spent $17,191 in state taxpayer money on a mailer that had the look and feel of a campaign flier. The mailing went out just days before a new ban . . . [that was] part of a package of ethics reforms that Obama takes credit for getting passed."

Obama objected to the story. It was pointed out that his campaign seemed to be trying to get away with something the law was meant to prevent.

Then, Obama did something that politicians rarely do—he backed down. He told the journalist, "I chewed out my staff for mailing that out when they did. It should have gone out a long time ago."

The problem seemed to be solved—that is, until the journalist talked with David Axelrod. According to Axelrod, his candidate had done nothing wrong. No laws were broken.

But Obama had admitted, earlier in the day, that the flyer should have gone out earlier, and Obama had even admitted to breaking the spirit of the law. Axelrod responded with utter amazement.

"He did?" Axelrod said. "He said that?"

The journalist replied, "Yes. How about that? It would appear that you have an honest man on your hands here."

"Yeah, I know. And you know what?" Axelrod said. "That can be a real problem."

In the final weeks of the primary campaign, the interest in Obama became intense. African Americans, especially, were eager to vote for him. Before Obama's television ads were shown, just fifteen percent of blacks said they planned to vote for him. A week after the first ad, that number jumped to fifty percent. The excitement was obvious. Obama now turned heads wherever he went. A fund-raiser thrown at a downtown bar was packed. It took Obama half an hour to push himself through the crowd to the back of the huge nightclub, where he was to speak.

Wherever Obama went in public as primary election day neared, he seemed excited too. "I am fired up!" he would exclaim before a joyous crowd. In private, however, Obama's ambition and the fact that he seemed very likely to become a U.S. senator was having a different effect—it was eating him up.

Not getting a job you want can be bad. But what about getting a job that you desperately want but that will change your life, whisk you away from your beloved wife and children, and cut short your time with close friends? Obama dearly loved his wife and his two young girls. He was beginning to realize that being a U.S. senator was going to take him away from them more than he might have thought.

A close friend threw a picnic for the campaign's volunteers and staff. Obama's face was tight and he was tense—very unlike him. His friend noticed this and asked him about it later. "Well, you are on your way now," she told him. "It looks like you are going to be a U.S. senator, and who knows what's next? So what's the matter, Barack?" When Obama lifted his head to answer, a tear rolled down his cheek. "I'm really going to miss those little girls," he said.

Election night was a wildly happy experience for most of Obama's supporters—for everyone except Obama. At the victory party, Obama paced around, checking notes for his speech, and greeting the many well-wishers who hugged him and shook his hand. He showed few signs that he was about to become the Democratic nominee for the U.S. Senate. "He's really pretty excited," Michelle told a writer for *Tribune*. "He's basically a calm guy. It takes a lot to push his buttons."

As David Axelrod looked over the election results, he began thinking about just what was happening. A black man was running away with a primary race for the U.S. Senate. The amount of support for Obama shocked even his chief advisers. "The most surprising and gratifying thing was when those numbers rolled in on primary night," Axelrod said. "What those numbers meant was . . . [that]

people were willing to look beyond race." The final tally: Obama had a whopping fifty-three percent of the vote. Hynes, the closest to him, had less than half of that.

One voter said that Obama was a "breath of fresh air." Others talked about Obama as a new kind of politician who brought a feeling of hope and honesty to the voters. "Truthfully, it feels like a movement," said a supporter. "I think for people of our generation, we haven't been a part of something like this before." Another supporter said, "When I first met him, I registered to vote that evening just so I could vote for him."

Back at his victory party, Obama walked onstage surrounded by his family—Michelle, Sasha and Malia; his brother-in-law, Craig Robinson; and his half sister Maya Soetoro-Ng. The Reverend Jesse Jackson was there as well. Obama told the crowd that they, not he, were responsible for this victory. He said that he was on a mission to change society, helping those who were the most vulnerable. "At its best, the idea of [the Democratic] party has been that we are going to expand opportunity and include people that have not been included, that we are going to give voice to the voiceless, and power to the powerless, and embrace people from the outside and bring them inside, and give them a piece of the American dream," Obama said.

Throughout his speech, a chant rose from the crowd: "Yes, we can! Yes, we can!"

15 The Ryan Files

Barack was nervous a couple times,
but he wowed them.
—Obama's campaign manager, Jim Cauley

Winning the primary was just the first step. All Obama had really won was a chance to run against a Republican in the general election. Within weeks of his win, Obama was on his way to Washington to raise cash for his new campaign.

People with power in Washington were all hearing about Obama, an exciting, up-and-coming African-American Democrat who could win votes from people of different races. Magazines such as *The New Yorker* and *The New Republic* wrote stories on him. He spent a couple of days and nights shaking hands, making small talk, and delivering speeches. In setting after setting, Obama's Harvard Law background and his reasonable tone impressed the crowd. "Barack was nervous a couple times, but he wowed them," Obama's campaign manager, Jim Cauley, said.

In his speeches now, Obama talked in a moderate manner instead of employing the fiery language he had used in the primary. Politicians often call this "moving to the middle," trying to convince voters that they are not too extreme. They try to appeal to as many people as possible.

Obama also hired new people to work for him, including Robert Gibbs as his communications director, the person who handles all the ways a candidate communicates with people outside the campaign, including how and when the candidate sees reporters and photographers. Gibbs quickly became very important to Obama. Only David Axelrod's advice mattered more to him. Gibbs could be charming and friendly, greeting people with a hearty smile and a friendly squeeze of the arm. But he could also be ruthless and didn't mind standing up to people or getting into arguments—things that Obama didn't particularly like doing. One person who worked for Obama's campaign said, "Robert is a bully." But the same person also admitted that "nine out of ten times, his gut instincts are right."

Gibbs was also one of the few aides on Obama's

staff who was fearless when it came to telling his boss he was wrong. He was not shy about reminding Obama to keep his speeches short and his answers to the point.

Republican voters in Illinois chose a candidate to run against Obama in the general election for the U.S. Senate. Jack Ryan was young, handsome, and wealthy. Early polls showed that Obama had a lead over him, but this seemed to be a matchup between two attractive candidates, both good on TV, but with very different ideas about government.

Ryan's campaign made an early mistake, however. They sent a young man with a video camera to follow Obama everywhere he went, hoping to catch him doing something embarrassing. It's not unusual for a politician to send someone with a camera to an opponent's speeches, looking for a mistake or a thoughtless comment. But the man from Ryan's campaign followed Obama everywhere he went, down hallways to the bathroom and along sidewalks to his car. Finally Obama's patience ran out. With his tracker in tow, Obama walked into a room full of reporters and announced to all of them, "Meet my stalker."

The next day's papers were filled with stories of this "stalker." People everywhere disapproved of what Ryan had done. A Ryan spokesman finally apologized to Obama.

Ryan's campaign ran into further trouble when a scandal about his divorce became public. Obama firmly refused to talk to reporters about the stories swirling around Ryan. "I've tried to make it clear throughout the campaign that my focus is on what I can do to help the families of Illinois and I'm not considering this something appropriate for me to comment on," he said again and again.

Within weeks, Ryan quit the race for Senate, leaving the Republican party adrift about what to do next. Meanwhile, things were going better and better for Obama. Axelrod, Cauley, Gibbs, and others were trying to get a spot for Obama to give a speech at the Democratic National Convention in Boston the next month. It was expected that John Kerry would be chosen there as the Democratic candidate for president. He had appeared together onstage with Obama once before and had been impressed by how calm and at ease Obama was while speaking to an audience. "Barack just killed at that event," said one of Obama's campaign workers. "You could see Kerry was looking at him with some awe."

At last Obama was offered the chance to give the keynote, or most important, speech on Tuesday night. Obama knew that he wanted to write the speech himself, without a lot of advice from others, even people who worked for him. Obama is a powerful speaker, but he is not at his best when he's reading something written by someone else. He knew that he spoke with much more honesty and directness when his words were all his own.

Obama wrote the speech along the campaign trail and in his hotel room in Springfield. Then he typed it into the computer at his home in Hyde Park in Chicago. Most of his writing was done between nine o'clock in the evening and one o'clock in the morning. This is usually his prized time alone, to catch some sports highlights on TV, to return email from friends, to write, to think. In the Obamas' Hyde Park house, there is a small room off the kitchen that Michelle calls "the Hole." This is Obama's writing and thinking spot, where he would disappear after they put their children to bed at night.

The words of the speech came fast. "It came out fairly easy," Obama said. "I had been thinking about these things for two years at that point." This was the moment Obama had been waiting for, his opportunity to convey his message of hope and togetherness to his biggest audience yet.

16 The Speech

*The pundits like to slice and dice our country
into red states and blue states; red states for
Republicans, blue states for Democrats. But I've got
news for them, too. . . . We are one people,
all of us pledging allegiance to the Stars and Stripes,
all of us defending the United States of America.*

—Barack Obama in his 2004 speech to
the Democratic National Convention

The fact that Obama was giving the keynote address of the Democratic National Convention meant a lot of people were going to be pay attention. It told the world that the Democratic party thought he was important. When Obama arrived in Boston that week, he was greeted as a celebrity. People predicted that by week's end Obama would either be a major star or a major dud.

Senator John Kerry of Massachusetts had won the Democratic nomination for president, and his name would be announced at the convention. He promised to make America "stronger at home and more respected abroad."

Obama arrived at his Boston hotel after midnight

on Sunday morning. Too excited to sleep, both he and his aides found themselves bumping into each other as they walked around in the hotel overnight. The next morning he was scheduled to appear on an important TV program, *Meet the Press*. The show's host was known for asking tough questions. Obama handled himself well, however, answering smoothly and getting his message in support of John Kerry across.

Over the next couple of days, Obama hopscotched through interviews, fund-raisers, and breakfasts, lunches, and dinners with powerful people. He could rarely take a few steps before being stopped by someone wanting an autograph, a well-wisher or a reporter. As Obama walked up to the set of another television show, the host offered him a hearty handshake. "You're the rock star now!" he said. Obama didn't agree. "Talk to my wife and she'll tell you that isn't so," he said.

Tuesday, the day of the keynote speech, was maddening. Obama had more than a dozen reporters and photographers keeping pace with his every step. His day began at six o'clock in the morning with a green-pepper omelet that aides had fetched from an all-night diner because the hotel restaurant had not yet opened. After several TV appearances, he had a second breakfast with other politicians from Illinois. There he said that his toughest critic, Michelle, had given a thumbs-up to his speech, or at least said that "I wasn't going to embarrass the Obama family."

Shortly after noon, Obama delivered a short speech at a rally. But he told the crowd he couldn't talk for long. "I can't throw out my throat for tonight or I've had it," he explained. As he came off the stage, a group of reporters mobbed him and insisted on an interview session. "I need five Baracks today," Obama's press secretary, Julian Green, said in frustration. "Everyone wants a piece of him. This is crazy, man."

After more TV interviews, Obama slipped away to grab a cup of tea at a Dunkin' Donuts counter. Immediately, reporters surrounded him. Obama gave up on the tea and answered questions for about five minutes before announcing that he had to use the restroom. The reporters trailed behind him. When Obama neared the portable toilets with the crowd still at his heels, he turned and said plaintively, "Can y'all just give me one moment to use the Port-O-Let?" But the group didn't back off until Julian Green threw out his arms, at last stopping them. "Guys, guys, guys!" Green shouted. "Can you let him use the Porta-Potty? Please! Thank you!" Soon,

Gibbs appeared with Obama's tea and whisked his boss away to practice the speech in private.

Obama had practiced the speech several times during the week. The final time Obama rehearsed it, Jim Cauley noticed that one listener had tears in her eyes. "Even that last try, though, Obama was only about eighty percent there," another observer said. "He didn't really nail it completely until he gave it before the crowd."

Obama began the keynote speech in the same fashion as his stump speeches, by introducing himself and his family ancestry—mother from Kansas, father from Kenya. He ended it by returning to his own life, saying that America's greatness lay in its ability to give hope to "a skinny kid with a funny name" like him. In between, he concentrated on the notion of a unifying force in America, a hope in the American Dream. He called it "the audacity of hope," meaning that it takes boldness and courage to hope that things will change for the better. Obama took that phrase straight from a sermon by his pastor, Jeremiah A. Wright, who himself had plucked it from writings by Dr. Martin Luther King Jr. (King had said, "I have the audacity to believe that peoples everywhere can have three meals a day for their bodies, education and culture for their minds, and dignity, quality, and freedom for their spirit. I believe that what self-centered men have torn down, other-centered men can build up.")

Audiences had reacted well to these lines in Obama's speeches while he was campaigning. One section of the keynote came directly from Obama's stump speech: "If there is a child on the South Side of Chicago who can't read, that matters to me, even if it's not my child. If there is a senior citizen somewhere who can't pay for their prescription drugs, and having to choose between medicine and the rent, that makes my life poorer, even if it's not my grandparent. If there's an Arab-American family being rounded up without benefit of an attorney . . . that threatens my civil liberties. . . . I am my brother's keeper. I am my sister's keeper. . . ."

John Kerry's staff had made one big change to Obama's speech when they read a draft. After Obama talked about the country being carved up into red states and blue states, he insisted that the country as a whole was "pledging allegiance to the red, white, *and* blue." But Kerry's people said they might want to use that line in Kerry's speech at the end of the week. Obama was "incredulous" at this request. "Of all the lines in the speech, Barack was the proudest of that one," David Axelrod said. But in the end, Obama changed his line to "pledging allegiance to the Stars and Stripes."

Arriving at Obama's messy hotel room before the speech, Axelrod and Gibbs realized that they had not considered an important part of that night. How should Obama dress? Obama was wearing one of his dark suits and a lightly patterned tie. The suit was fine, but when Axelrod took a close look at the tie, they both felt he needed to change it. Obama defended his choice of tie. When he sought Michelle's opinion, however, she agreed with the two men. So that was that—the search for a new tie was on. Finally Axelrod spotted Gibbs's brand-new baby-blue striped tie. This would do well. "But this is my tie," Gibbs protested. "I bought it specifically for tonight." It would now be Obama's tie.

Obama had never spoken before such a big audience: five thousand people. Huddled with his small team behind the stage, Obama, who had been calm throughout the week, suddenly felt nervous. But he did not fail to delight the crowd. He stumbled a bit in the opening lines. But after he mentioned that his mother was from Kansas, audience members from

Kansas erupted in a cheer. You could see a jolt of energy rush through Obama's body. He had made that special audience connection.

Soon his audience was simply enraptured. "There's not a liberal America and a conservative America—there's the *United States* of America," Obama said clearly. "There's not a black America and white America and Latino America and Asian America—there's the *United States* of America. . . . We are one people. . . ." Democrats of all races and ages nodded. Some were crying. Many shrieked and jumped from their seats. Backstage, Michelle had tears glistening on her cheeks. "When I looked past the stage," Julian Green remembered later, "and saw how people reacted, when I saw . . . people crying, I thought to myself that I had never experienced anything like this, anything this powerful. You know, I'm not sure what this means, but I couldn't help but think, 'Is he the one? Could he really be the one we have been looking for?'"

When Obama finished, Michelle dashed onto the stage and patted her husband on the back. They waved as she guided him backstage. Obama flashed a self-satisfied smile at Green. "I guess it was a pretty good speech, huh?" Obama said.

The next day, as Obama was riding up on an

escalator, a woman riding down next to him beamed. As the two passed each other, she leaned over and said to Obama, "I just cannot wait until you are president."

17 Back to Illinois

This guy is real. The others are phony.
—A man listening to a speech by Obama

Back in Illinois, Barack Obama still had an election to win. However, it was now nearly August and Obama had no Republican challenger. That might seem good, but it's hard to run a campaign when you don't know who your foe is. So Obama kept pushing his staff, and his staff kept pushing him. "Jimmy, I don't want to hear any of this 'We don't have an opponent' stuff," Obama told his campaign manager, Jim Cauley. "We have to keep running hard."

Obama's staff wanted to make sure the voters of Illinois knew that Obama was still focused on their needs. So they planned a statewide campaign tour to begin the weekend after he returned home. So, still exhausted after Boston, Obama started off on a sixteen-hundred-mile trip around the state. He visited thirty-nine cities in just five days.

Obama wanted to spend time with his family after the convention. His staff rented a recreational vehicle so Michelle and his daughters could come along. But with eight events each day, it was hard to fit in family time.

Everywhere Obama went he was greeted by big excited crowds. "Apparently, the speech turned out okay Tuesday," he said with a grin to a group of about five hundred. "But the reason I was there was because of you, the voters of Illinois. People didn't care that I was from a different town or that I was a different color."

There was a part of Obama, whose father had abandoned him as a child and whose mother traveled to faraway places and left him with his grandparents, that clearly enjoyed the public attention. He loved to connect with an audience. On his first tour speech, as the crowd roared, Obama blurted out, "I love you all! Love ya!"

And they seemed to return the feeling. "I vote for people, and not for political reasons, and this man inspires me," one listener explained. This man said he would vote again for George W. Bush for president—and for Obama for senator, even though the two men held political views that were opposite in almost every way. "He can really get your juices flowing," he said. "This guy is real. The others are phony." In another town, a woman held up a sign: IF YOU HAVE A DREAM, VOTE FOR OBAMA.

Richard Durbin, the senior senator from Illinois, came along on several days of the trip. Durbin was considered one of the most serious members of the Senate, and he had earned great respect in Washington. But he wasn't the kind of person who attracts much attention. Before one event on the tour, Obama was busy with phone calls and told Durbin that he would meet him there. Durbin replied that he would rather just wait until Obama was ready. "I can't go there without you," he explained. "Nobody will have any clue who I am unless I walk in next to you."

Obama spoke about giving everyday people a greater voice in Washington. He wanted to put an end to bickering between the two political parties. He promised voters that he was running for their sake, not his own. And Obama also took a strong stand against the Iraq War. "When we send our men off to war, we need to make sure we are sending them off to the right war," he told audiences, who reacted enthusiastically.

As the days wore on, the crowds seemed to grow even bigger. Once Obama stepped from his SUV and was swallowed up by a sea of several hundred admirers, each wanting to shake his hand or give him a hug or take a photo. "Someone is going to have to go in and fish him out," one aide grumbled. "How can you not let all of this go to your head?"

After a couple of days of fighting the crowds, Obama was starting to grow more tired. Each event ran long because he would have to sign autographs and shake hands with hundreds of adoring fans. Finally, on the third day, a police officer threw one of Obama's young aides a roll of police line tape and told him, "Keep it and use it, son." Obama's staff started using the tape to keep the crowds away from Obama. Obama apologized to audiences that he could not stay longer, sign autographs, and meet each one of them.

Aides took Sasha and Malia to theme parks or water parks for the day, bringing them back to their parents at hotels at night. But in the evenings Obama was still speaking at fund-raisers and rallies. So much for the family trip. "When are we going to see our children again?" Obama asked Michelle one morning. "I'm not sure," she replied.

As the caravan made its way back to Chicago, nearly everyone involved in the tour was ready for its end. After giving his final speech and posing for a photo, Obama called over the lead organizer of the trip, a law student named Jeremiah Posedel. Obama placed his hands on Posedel's shoulders and then fixed a serious gaze directly into the young man's eyes. "You did a great job and I am so appreciative of all the work you've done," Obama told him. "But don't ever . . . do that to me again."

In early August, the Republican party in Illinois chose Alan Keyes as its candidate for the Senate. Keyes, who was then living in Maryland, was a former talk show host who had run for president twice. An African-American conservative, Keyes was best known for his rousing speaking style. He was fiery and not the least bit shy about attacking any opponent.

Obama and Keyes were both part of Chicago's yearly Bud Billiken Parade, which runs through the city's South Side. It's called the largest African-American parade in the country, running for several miles along Martin Luther King Drive. Thousands of parade-goers waved blue-and-white Obama signs, wore Obama stickers, and shrieked as his float passed by. They chanted "O-ba-ma! O-ba-ma! O-ba-ma!"

Keyes, however, was on foot at the back of the

parade. As he shook hands and walked along, watchers booed and hissed. One man briefly grabbed his arm and warned him to go back to Maryland. A wild-eyed woman ran up to him, lifted an Obama sign above her head and screamed in his face, "Obama for president! Obama for president!"

Through the next several months, Keyes attacked Obama for his support of abortion rights. At one point, he said that if Jesus could vote in Illinois, he would cast a ballot against Obama. When Obama ran across Keyes at another parade in Chicago, he rushed over and tried to talk to him. Obama hates conflict, and he thought that the two of them could have a reasonable discussion. "Barack thinks he can win over anyone," Jim Cauley observed. But before long, Obama and Keyes were arguing, and the argument got worse when Obama, trying to calm things down, put his hand on Keyes's shoulder. Axelrod told Obama, "You know, Barack, you can't hug a porcupine without getting pricked."

For the rest of the campaign, Obama kept his hands off the porcupine and didn't try to talk to Keyes. That November he won the general election for Senate, defeating Keyes by seventy percent to twenty-nine percent.

◆ ◆ ◆

The final celebration party for Obama's election victory was not as exciting as might have been expected. Most people had expected Obama to win his race, and their eyes were on the presidential contest between John Kerry and President Bush. When Kerry, the Democratic candidate, lost, Obama's Democratic partygoers were depressed. Obama himself was so tired that his victory speech was rather flat. But that was of little concern. He had won the election.

And Obama's family no longer needed to worry about money. Obama had received nearly two million dollars to write three books, including a children's book to be cowritten with Michelle. Upon hearing this, Michelle had to admit that she had been wrong before. Obama's plan for success had worked. He had won a Senate seat and now would write a book that would keep his family secure for a long time. He had climbed the beanstalk and had indeed come down with the golden egg. "I can't believe you pulled this off," Michelle told him. For a man who had never tried to get rich, Obama was now more than well off. "I am not looking for money," Obama had told Jim Cauley. "All I'm looking for is a decent house and the ability to send my little girls to whatever school I want." He had reached those goals.

18 The Senator

Congratulations, Mr. Senator.
—Michelle Obama

The week that Barack Obama officially became a senator, in January 2005, appeared to be a time of joy for him and his family. Senators must swear an oath of office, a solemn promise to do their duty in their jobs. After Obama took the oath, he, Michelle, and the two girls strolled across the Capitol grounds to the Library of Congress, where he would greet a party of well-wishers. Obama and Michelle clasped hands. "Congratulations, Mr. Senator," Michelle said with a soft kiss. "Congratulations, Madame Senator," Obama answered with a warm smile.

With a handful of reporters trailing along to capture the scene, six-year-old Malia looked up at her father and asked, "Daddy, are you going to be president?" Obama glanced at the reporters and didn't answer.

As Obama reached the Library of Congress, his party guests were waiting in line. Obama's half sister, Maya, and her husband had traveled from Hawaii. Obama ran up to the Reverend Jesse Jackson, who gave him a bear hug. "I'm not a toy senator. I'm not a play senator!" Obama said. "I'm a real senator now!"

Inside, Obama told his audience that his mission to create a fairer, more just America had only begun. "We are going to be working hard to make sure that every child gets a decent shot at life and to make sure that every senior citizen is cared for, that the diversity of this country is appreciated and to make sure that we create the kind of nation that these children and your children and your grandchildren deserve," he declared. "I promise you that this is not the end of the road."

Obama hired Pete Rouse, who was familiar with the ways Washington worked, to run his Senate office. The first thing on his list was to make a plan for his first two years in the Senate. By 2005 his advisers knew that Obama had a shot at being chosen for vice president or perhaps even running for president. The day after his election to the Senate, Obama had flatly denied that he would run for president in 2008. But other politicians had said that and then changed their minds.

According to "the Plan," Obama should spend his first quarter of a year in the Senate hiring staff, learning the names and faces of Washington, and writing his book. He also wanted to get less attention from the media. This was the hardest thing to accomplish. His communications director, Robert Gibbs, spent most of his time turning down requests for interviews rather than seeking them out.

The Plan called for Obama to spend most of his first year making sure that voters in Illinois knew he was taking care of their needs. He went to nearly forty meetings with voters in his home state in 2005. Obama also took foreign trips in this first year. He had been selected for the Foreign Relations Committee, a group of senators whose job is to oversee the laws and treaties that govern how the United States deals with other countries. Obama visited Russia, Eastern Europe, and the Middle East, including Israel and Iraq. Then, in 2006, the Plan said that Obama would try to raise money to help Democrats win more seats in Congress. In the second half of that year he would visit his father's homeland of East Africa and his second book would hit the bookstores.

Obama's first few months in Washington were

especially difficult. He had wanted to bring Michelle and the girls to live with him there. But nearly everyone advised him to keep his family in Chicago. Michelle's mother and her closest friends still lived there. She still worked at the University of Chicago Hospitals. Besides, Obama would be traveling back to Illinois every week. After some time, Obama realized that it would be best to rent an apartment in Washington and spend Tuesday through Thursday nights there. He usually had a full schedule back in Illinois the rest of the week, but Sundays would now be devoted to his family.

Soon, another problem developed with the Plan. Writing a book is a full-time job in itself. And writing one while learning a new job is incredibly difficult. "I'm writing a book and I just don't have any time in my life," Obama complained. Throughout his first year in the Senate, it was easy to see that Obama was tired. Once he nearly fell asleep while giving a speech. As he stood at the edge of the stage, holding a microphone, his eyes fell shut for a moment and his knees wobbled while he was talking to the crowd.

His friends noticed a difference in him. "Does he look happy to you?" one asked. "I think the job looked better on paper to him." Dan Shomon, his former Springfield aide, said that Obama "has no time for himself and no life. . . . He can't go play poker . . . or get enough time with his family—and that's the downside, a big downside. His life is over, and I keep thinking, you know, he really didn't ask for this." Another aide made a similar comment. "He has to watch himself wherever he goes. . . . He doesn't have time to be himself except when he is with Michelle. He always has to be 'on.'"

Obama also became careful to avoid any kind of controversy, or issues about which people might strongly disagree with him. Some complained that Obama was no longer liberal enough. But Obama said he was just following his beliefs. "I think that what you've seen are times where I've actually done what I think is best, but you know, there may be some folks who disagree and automatically assume that I've done it for political purposes," he explained.

On difficult matters or when he wasn't sure how to vote, Obama would call his staff into his office and lead debates about how to proceed. "And he just loves to have us argue it out in front of him," said one staffer. But this staffer also said that Obama was his own man when it came to making tough votes. The staff might leave the room thinking he would vote one way, but he could just as easily go the other.

Obama did not do much to call attention to himself in his first year. But there were two events in 2005 where he did catch everybody's eye.

In June at Knox College, a small school in Illinois, Obama (who admits he was nervous) delivered his first major speech as a U.S. senator. It let everyone listening know what he intended to do as senator. Mentioning moments in American history like the abolition of slavery and the civil rights movement, Obama said that America's success is built on a sense that we must take care of each other. And this is the surest way to make sure the country continues to prosper. And, Obama added, the best means for looking out for each other is through government: strengthening public schools, providing health care to all, asking people to devote time to helping others rather than only thinking about making money.

He said that there are those who believe the way for a country to do well is for everyone to look out for him- or herself. "It's a tempting idea, because it doesn't require much thought or ingenuity. It allows us to say to those whose health care or tuition may rise faster than they can afford—tough luck. It allows us to say to the Maytag workers who have lost their job—life isn't fair. It lets us say to the child who was born into poverty—pull yourself up by your boot-straps. . . . But there is a problem. It won't work. It ignores our history." Obama went on to say that America has prospered not only because people have worked hard and done their best, but also because we have taken care of each other. "The idea that everybody has a stake in the country, that we're all in it together and everybody's got a shot at opportunity"—this is what has made America strong and secure.

Obama's speech at Knox didn't get a lot of attention from reporters. But the speech sped across the internet, drawing cheers from liberals. Conservatives, however, looked at this speech and realized that even though Obama patiently listened to them, he was not one of them.

Obama's second attention-getting moment of 2005 came after Hurricane Katrina caused flooding and devastation in New Orleans and along the coast of Louisiana and Mississippi. More than a thousand people were killed; tens of thousands lost their homes. The people worst off were mostly poor and mostly black. Many thought the U.S. government did not do enough to help them, and some charged that racism was the reason.

Obama agreed to appear on a TV show, *This Week with George Stephanopoulos*, to speak on the tragedy of Hurricane Katrina. The interviewer asked Obama if racism was the reason why the government had not responded better to the terrible tragedy.

Obama responded in a typically careful, balanced way. "I think that the entire country felt shame about what had happened. Now, my general attitude has been that the incompetence by . . . the Department of Homeland Security and by this administration was color-blind." In other words, Obama didn't believe that the Republican government under George Bush let black people suffer on purpose. But he went on to say that the tragedy of the hurricane was made worse because the people who were supposed to be in charge didn't understand what life is like for the poor and for minorities, and that lack of understanding or caring led to bad decisions. "What I do think is that whoever was in charge of planning was so detached from the realities of inner-city life in a place like New Orleans that they couldn't conceive of the notion that somebody couldn't load up their SUV, put one hundred dollars' worth of gas in there, put [in] some sparkling water, and drive off to a hotel and check in with a credit card." Obama went on, "I think that the important thing for us now is to recognize that we have situations in America in which race continues to play a part, that class continues to play a part." He said that everyone in the country does not have the same chances. "When disaster strikes, it tears the curtain away from the . . . problems that we have beneath them, and black and white, all of us should be concerned to make sure that that's not the kind of America that's reflected on our television screens."

Obama's careful language was in contrast to the anger and frustration vented by other black leaders. The Reverend Jesse Jackson was concerned that younger black people, who did not live through times before the civil rights movement, might not see racism when it was in front of them. "I was jailed [for] trying to use the public library. I remember blacks being drafted for World War II and you couldn't vote," Jackson said, reminding listeners that it was the struggles of the civil rights movement that had made it possible for Obama to achieve his success.

Obama said calmly, "Not everybody's going to serve the same role. . . . Reverend Jackson or Reverend [Al] Sharpton is going to have a different role to play than someone like myself, who's representing all sorts of people. . . . I actually have felt very comfortable speaking on issues that are of particular importance to the African-American community, without losing focus on my primary task, which is to represent all the people of Illinois. . . . I think that on every issue . . . if I'm speaking honestly, if I'm speaking what I think, then usually things turn out all right."

19 South Africa

I realize that I offer these words of hope at a time
when hope seems to have gone from many parts of the
world. As we speak, there is slaughter in Darfur. There is
war in Iraq. . . . And I have to admit, it makes me wonder
sometimes whether men are in fact capable of learning
from history. . . . And then I thought that if
a black man of African descent would return to his
ancestors' homeland as a United States senator, and
would speak to a crowd of black and white South
Africans who shared the same freedoms and
the same rights, . . . things do change
and history does move forward.
—Barack Obama, Cape Town, South Africa, August 2006

Barack Obama's journey to Africa was designed to
be various things: a way for the new senator to learn
about the continent, a family visit to his relatives in
Kenya and, perhaps most important, something to
keep TV, newspapers, magazines, and radio full of
stories about Obama. It was part of the Plan that
Obama and his advisers had worked out for Obama's
first two years in the Senate.

Reporters were especially excited about the trip
because of the astounding success of *Dreams from*

My Father. A large part of that book was about Obama's travels to Kenya to study his African heritage and connect with his Kenyan relatives. In August 2006, people were fascinated with Obama's life story. This trip was another way for them to explore his history. There were swarms of Kenyan, American, and international reporters recording Obama's every move.

But Obama did have things he wanted to accomplish in Africa that were not about keeping his name in the news. Among other worries, he was deeply concerned about the horrors of the civil war in the Darfur region of Sudan. Thousands of Sudanese were being killed there each month and millions more were being driven from their homes. Obama didn't have specific solutions to offer, but he believed that the United States should be paying more attention to the conflict there.

"Kenya will just be crazy—the media, the people, everything will be insane," Obama's communications director, Robert Gibbs, said. As usual, his instinct was exactly right. The fifteen-day trip would include visits to five countries, but most of the journey was to be spent in South Africa and then Kenya. After Kenya, Obama had planned brief visits to the Congo, Djibouti, and the Darfur region of Sudan.

But Kenya, the homeland of Obama's father, would be the high point of the trip. Since Obama's election to the U.S. Senate, he had become a hero in that East African nation, especially among his father's native tribe, the Luo. A beer named for Obama was sold there; a school was named in his honor; and a play based on his *Dreams* books had been performed at the Kenyan National Theater.

After arriving in Cape Town in South Africa, Obama's first trip was a boat ride to Robben Island. On this island, Nelson Mandela spent eighteen of his twenty-seven years in prison for fighting against the government's unjust and racist system of apartheid. As he would be on the whole trip, Obama was followed by reporters from newspapers and magazines and two crews filming stories for TV.

The ferry pushed off from the Cape Town harbor, and Obama settled into a seat next to his guide for the day, Ahmed Kathrada. Also a fighter against apartheid, Kathrada was a friend of Mandela's and had spent eighteen years in jail on Robben Island as well. He told Obama about the history of the prison. When Mandela and Kathrada were kept there, prisoners had almost no contact with the outside world. They did not even know when the first spaceship landed on the moon. They were allowed to send only one letter (about two pages long) every six months. Lighter-skinned prisoners of Asian background like Kathrada were treated a little better than darker-skinned Africans.

Once the boat docked, Obama and Kathrada walked to the now empty prison. The two men stepped down the narrow hallways and quickly reached Mandela's cramped prison cell. Several photographers snapped pictures of Obama, looking thoughtful, peering out the window from behind the steel bars.

On his second day in Cape Town Obama visited a community health center that mostly treated AIDS patients. In 2006 in South Africa, one in five people in the country—nearly five million—were infected with HIV, the virus that causes AIDS. South Africa's leaders had been criticized for not doing enough to stop the spread of AIDS and for making public statements about the disease that were not backed up with scientific evidence.

The health center that Obama visited was located in Khayelitsha, a poor area with miles and miles of tin-roofed shacks. Outside the clinic, Obama was asked by reporters to speak about South Africa's AIDS crisis and what should be done to deal with it. Obama charged that the government was in "denial" about AIDS. He urged people in government to take the problem seriously and to tell the truth about the disease and how it can be spread. "It's not an issue of Western science versus African science," he said. "It's just science, and it's not right." He then announced that he would take an AIDS test when he reached Kenya. Many people in Africa believe AIDS to be a shameful disease, and some would rather die than get tested; Obama hoped to show with his actions that there was no shame in getting the test.

Before this, few leaders had spoken out so firmly on the way the South African government was handling the AIDS crisis. "We wish more politicians were that honest," said one of South Africa's AIDS activists.

That afternoon, Obama met with Desmond Tutu, a winner of the Nobel Peace Prize. An archbishop of the Anglican church, Tutu was a fighter against apartheid and now works to help those with AIDS. In a brief appearance before reporters, Tutu praised his visitor and mentioned that he thought Obama would make a good candidate for president. Tutu also joked, "I hope that I would be equally nice to a young white senator." After Obama chuckled, Tutu added, "But I am glad you are black."

Back in Cape Town that evening, Obama gave a speech. As he often does, he spoke of how human beings everywhere are connected. But here in South Africa, the bond he described was not just among good-hearted Americans but among well-meaning people all over the world. He said modern threats such as AIDS, the spread of nuclear weapons, terrorism, and environmental problems should bring people together, not divide them. Finally he said that his very presence in Africa—a black senator from the United States—provided living proof that humanity was moving forward.

Obama had hoped for a meeting with South Africa's president, Thabo Mbeki. On his third day in South Africa, Obama learned that Mbeki would not meet with him. Mbeki was one of the politicians in South Africa who did not seem concerned about how AIDS was harming the country. He had even questioned whether HIV infection leads to AIDS, a scientific fact known the world over. Obama wondered if his criticism of the way the government was dealing with the AIDS crisis was part of the reason Mbeki refused to see him. On that day, Obama also learned that he would not be able to visit the Congo iolence that had erupted there following residential election.

Obama spoke to reporters that evening. He told them that he had been careful not to criticize the United States while he traveled abroad, but said he could feel in South Africa that people's feelings about the United States were not always positive. America's decision to invade Iraq, Obama said, was responsible for that. "So I think there is a lot of work that we're going to have to do in the coming years" to change people's minds, he added.

On the fourth day, Obama drove to Soweto, a suburb of the city of Johannesburg. In June 1976, there had been riots there called the Soweto Uprising when the white government declared that black students would only be educated in the Afrikaans language, not in English. A museum in Soweto tells about the uprising and its most famous victim, Hector Pieterson, a thirteen-year-old who was killed when police fired at protesting students. With Hector's sister, Antoinette, as his guide, Obama toured the Pieterson museum.

Antoinette and Obama stopped in front of a photo big enough to cover a wall. It showed the body of Antoinette's brother Hector as he was carried from the protest in the arms of another young man. In the photo, seventeen-year-old Antoinette runs alongside the man holding her dead brother. In the museum,

Obama put an arm around Antoinette's shoulders and she put an arm around his waist. The two lingered in front of the huge photo as cameras flashed behind them.

Outside, in a light rain, Obama gave a short speech as he stood with Antoinette before a memorial to her brother. He mentioned that he had first become interested in politics in college when he protested apartheid, just as activists in South Africa were doing at the same time. "If it wasn't for some of the activities here I might not have been involved in politics," he said.

20 Nairobi

This is where he belongs. He just goes there
to work [in America], but he should and will come
back home to be one of our own.

—A Kenyan woman

The next day, Obama arrived at the airport in Nairobi, Kenya. When he landed, about a hundred people started gathering in small groups along the roadway near the airport. They were strangely quiet and were all looking toward a building in the front of the airport. In a hushed voice, a man explained, "Obama is here."

After taking a few moments for photos inside a small back room, Obama walked outside. More people had gathered. They stood under palm trees and along curbs, and one man hoisted a little girl onto his shoulders. When Obama came through the doors, the crowd simply stood and watched in silence. Walking up to the car he would use, Obama waved stiffly and flashed a smile before he ducked into the SUV.

That night, in his hotel, Obama gave interviews for TV. His communications director, Robert Gibbs, warned reporters that the trip might get a little frantic. "I'm not sure if you folks were at the airport," he said. "But we're going to find that even when things are not advertised, some Kenyans will gather. What we learned today—expect the unexpected," he finished. "Now the fun begins."

The next morning Obama and his family appeared at the Nairobi State House for a ceremony to welcome him. The event was held outside under a tent. Dozens of embassy workers wore orange-and-yellow T-shirts with OBAMA IN THE HOUSE on the front. Songs had been written for Obama's visit, and a group of clapping and finger-snapping Kenyans sang, "When you see Obama has come to Kenya, this day is blessed." As Obama began his speech, he was interrupted by his eight-year-old daughter, Malia, who shouted, "Daddy, Daddy, look at me!"

Obama met government officials that morning at the state house, including Kenyan president Mwai Kibaki. Kibaki had won his election by promising to end corruption, the way that people who worked for government or business took bribes and used their jobs to get money for themselves. But more than three years later, corruption was still a problem. Many Kenyans were gloomy about their country and its leadership. "People have just kind of given up on the government," said a reporter. "They feel we'll never get what we want." In his meeting with Kibaki, Obama and the president discussed the importance of clean government.

Obama's next stop was a meeting at a restaurant. Outside, workers had left their jobs to crowd atop balconies, huddle in doorways, and press against the iron fences around the building. Reporters talked with them, asking how they felt about Obama. Some thought of him as a Kenyan who had risen to great power in the United States. He gave them hope that they or their children could succeed in their own daily lives. Others imagined that Obama would make the world pay more attention to Kenya. Some even believed that he would bring riches to Kenya from the United States. This last group thought that Obama truly belonged in Kenya, not America.

One woman said firmly that Obama would choose to leave America and live in Kenya: "This is where he belongs. He just goes there to work [in America], but he should and will come back home to be one of our own." When asked why she believed Obama would come to live in Kenya, she continued: "Because the father is a Kenyan. You know, your father is your bloodline; it's not your mother—it is your father. So you belong where your father comes from, in your fatherland. Kenya is in his blood." Another man saw Obama as a sign that the United States had overcome racism. "If the Americans can select a senator like Obama," he said, "that means that Americans embrace the whole world and they are true democrats. There is no racism there."

After lunch, Obama visited the memorial that had been set up at the former site of the U.S. Embassy. The building had been bombed in 1998, killing nearly 250 people. The deadly bombing was done by people connected with the terrorists who attacked the United States on September 11, 2001. Dozens of people, including Michelle, Sasha, and Malia, stood there waiting for Obama. Obama shook the hands of a long row of people, with Michelle nearly last in line. Michelle smiled and held out her hand, as if she were just another member of the greeting party. "I'm your wife, welcome," she said with a warm smile. "Hello, wife," Obama said with a playful grin.

On the memorial were the names of those killed in the attack, along with these words: MAY THE INNOCENT VICTIMS OF THIS TRAGIC EVENT REST IN THE KNOWLEDGE THAT IT HAS STRENGTHENED OUR RESOLVE TO WORK FOR A WORLD IN WHICH MAN IS ABLE TO LIVE ALONGSIDE HIS BROTHER IN PEACE. A large crowd had gathered in the street. Workers in a seven-story office building nearby leaned out of big windows to watch as Obama signed a guest book and laid a wreath gently at the foot of the memorial.

After the brief ceremony, Obama went inside a nearby building to chat with people from the government and the embassy while Sasha and Malia played outside. Michelle walked about, watching them. Then a roar went up from the crowd. Michelle was startled. "Oh my goodness! What was that?" she exclaimed. When she heard that it was for her husband, who must have walked outside the building, she replied, "Oh, my! For Barack?"

The crowds in the streets were cheering, standing on cars, dancing, whistling and screaming, and waving their arms wildly. The people were chanting: "Obama, come to us! Obama, come to us!" Obama was shaking hands with members of the crowd. With each step he took toward the street, the chanting got louder. "Obama, come to us! Obama, come to us!"

The legend of Obama was growing by leaps and bounds. Indeed, the Plan was going exactly as everyone had hoped.

After a couple of minutes, Robert Gibbs grabbed Obama's sleeve and told him to head back to a waiting car. Then Gibbs noticed a young man holding up an eye-catching portrait of Obama, painted in brown, black, gold, and white. Beneath Obama's image were the words WARUAKI DAL, or WELCOME HOME. Gibbs grabbed the man's arm and led him back to Obama's SUV. Then Gibbs introduced the two. Gregory Ochieng, the young man with the painting, came from a country village near the farm of Obama's relatives. Obama accepted Ochieng's painting and thanked him.

Ochieng, a member of the Luo tribe, told several reporters that he felt a deep connection to Obama because Obama's father had been a Luo. "He is my tribesman," Ochieng explained. "I feel happy that a Kenyan is representing us in the U.S. as a senator. So when I heard he was coming here, I thought of doing something that was unique." Asked by reporters if his meeting with Obama had been as good as he had hoped, he said with a broad smile, "It is better."

Obama's next event was a news conference,

where he would speak to reporters. The audience filled a ballroom at a downtown hotel. Every journalist in Africa seemed to be there. Wearing a pin on his jacket that combined the flags of Kenya and the United States, Obama stood behind a brown wooden lectern.

Obama opened the news conference by recognizing that this visit was remarkably different from his earlier trips to Kenya. This time, he wanted to be a "bridge between the two nations." "Part of my role," he said, "is to communicate how much the American people appreciate the Kenyan people and how much they value the partnership that the United States has with Kenya. Part of it, I think, is also to listen and find out what is on the minds of the Kenyan people. . . . Part of my goal is also to maybe highlight some of the values and ideals of the United States that I think might be helpful to the Kenyan people."

Obama also spoke about the importance of honesty and speaking out against crime and corruption.

> I think that there's a tendency . . . to not want to speak out against fellow Africans. . . . And I think we've moved beyond that; I think the time is now, where we have to

understand that nobody in Africa wants to be bullied. . . . Nobody wants to be tortured to death because of speaking their mind. Nobody wants to have to pay a bribe in order to get a business or get a job or just go about their daily business. And it's incumbent upon us, when we see those things happening, to speak up. . . . That kind of honesty will improve governments everywhere.

Back at the hotel, Obama spoke again to reporters. Despite his incredible popularity in Kenya, he reminded everyone that the fate of the country was in the hands of the Kenyans themselves. "Kenya is not my country. It's the country of my father," Obama said. "I feel a connection, but ultimately, it's not going to be me, it's going to be them who are climbing a path to improving their new lives."

21 Siaya: A Father's Home

It's not just God we praise, but Obama too.
—Elderly Kenyan women chanting to Obama

This was Obama's third trip to see his father's family. He had first visited just after college and then again after finishing Harvard Law School. The family farm was near a town called Kolego in the Siaya district of Nyanza province. Siaya was home to various small farming and trading villages. Most of the people who lived there were poor, with more than half living on less than a dollar a day. The district's largest city was Kisumu. Almost all the people in the area were from the Luo tribe.

On his earlier visits, Obama had gotten on a train in Nairobi and ridden it through the night and the morning to Kisumu. When he arrived, he had walked half a mile to a bus station by himself and had been greeted by a handful of relatives. Obama talked about the difference to reporters. "The last time I arrived in my grandmother's village, there was a goat in my lap and some chickens," he said. This time he arrived into Kisumu after a forty-minute plane ride.

When Obama's flight landed, a mass of people seemed to appear out of thin air. The enthusiastic crowd turned out to be mostly Peace Corps workers from the United States. Obama was loaded into an SUV and driven to the New Nyanza Provincial General Hospital, where he and Michelle were to take their AIDS tests. It was Saturday, and along the sides of these roads were markets selling everything from fruit to American T-shirts to Air Jordan basketball shoes. Every Kisumu street was lined with waving, hollering, and overjoyed people, hoping to catch a glimpse of Obama.

At the hospital, thousands had turned out to see Obama. People stood on rooftops of the hospital buildings, sat along balconies and climbed into trees. Some wore T-shirts bearing Obama's name or image. Others held up pictures of him or waved flags with his name or face.

Obama and Michelle headed for a mobile clinic and disappeared inside to thunderous applause. After the husband and wife got their fingertips pricked to draw small samples of blood, Obama stepped outside to speak. He took a microphone in his left hand and held up his right arm to ask for quiet. But the mass of people drowned him out and began to push forward. Obama urged calm. "Stop pushing, no pushing," he implored. But no one paid attention. Obama sat down on the top step. "This is . . ." he said, pausing to find just the right word. "This is interesting."

This next stop was at a project run by CARE Kenya, an organization that fights poverty. Obama had made donations to the project, which gave money to women who care for orphans, allowing them to buy things they need, such as sewing machines. To reach the event, buses and cars carrying Obama and reporters drove over uneven and unpaved roads, chugging by tiny green farms with thatch huts that had mud or tin roofs.

The buses finally arrived at an event that was set amid a deep green thicket of trees and dust. About a hundred and fifty Kenyans, many in traditional African clothing, gathered to be part of a ceremony in Obama's honor. Most were women and children. A handful of the older women danced and sang, in Luo, "It's not just God we praise, but Obama too." Obama danced with them and gave a quick speech, calling the event "a wonderful homecoming."

Michelle also stood up and danced in a circle with the Luo women. But she was still trying to understand the way her husband was adored in Kenya. "It's all a bit overwhelming," she confessed. "It's hard to interpret what all of this means and what it means to us as a family." She went on, "This doesn't really make me think of Barack Obama and his fame and fortune. It makes you think of what you can do to help here. . . . The spectacle is interesting, but in the end, this has to be all about more than Barack Obama."

Next was the main event of the day—and perhaps the entire trip: Obama's visit to his father's farm. Obama didn't know that Raila Odinga, a candidate for president of Kenya, had gathered thousands of Luo for a political festival in Obama's honor. Local politicians and people who worked with them had gathered to see Obama. A group of schoolchildren appeared outside the schoolhouse named for him. They stood in a long row, swaying their hips and waving their arms rhythmically to a song composed for their American visitor. The familiar words of "This Land Is Your Land" had been changed to mention Kenyan landmarks: "This land is your land, this land is my land, from Lake Victoria to the Coastal Province, from Nairobi to the Rift Valley, this land is my land alone."

Obama had given donations to the Senator Obama Kogelo Secondary School, so the school had been able to buy chalkboards and wooden desks and science equipment. But the building did not seem to have running water. The classrooms had concrete floors and worn wooden tables and chairs. "Hopefully, I can provide some assistance in the future to this school and all that it can be," Obama said.

At the political ceremony organized by Odinga, the Luo Council of Elders sat in white lawn chairs underneath a long row of canvas tents, wearing brightly colored robes over their suits and ties. Speaking in Luo, Odinga opened the event with a speech. It was then Obama's turn. He stepped onto a wooden table and grabbed the microphone. But instead of talking about his own life, he told the crowd his father's life story:

> As I was driving up here, I thought about my father. Some of you may be aware, I didn't know him that well. He actually did come back here to Kenya. I was the one . . . back in the United States. . . . It wasn't until as an adult that I came to visit this area. I

remember the first time that I came, I thought to myself that even though I grew up on the other side of the world . . . when I came here I felt the spirit among the people that told me I belonged. Everybody was so warm and so gracious and so friendly and hospitable. One of the things that you realize about this area is that even though a lot of times people don't have a lot, they are willing to give you what they have. . . . As I traveled through here, one of the things I realized is how remarkable it was the journey my father had traveled. He grew up around here. He was taking care of goats for my grandfather. And maybe sometimes he would go to a school not so different from Senator Barack Obama's school, except maybe it was smaller and they had even less in terms of equipment and books. And teachers were paid even less and sometimes there wasn't enough money to go to school full-time. Yet despite all that . . . the community lifted him up and gave him the opportunity to go to secondary school and then go to a university in America and then get a Ph.D. from Harvard and then come back here and work with

many of the individuals who are here today. It's a story of what's possible when a community comes together and supports its children.

After Obama finished, the moment of the day was at hand. He was off to visit his father's farm and his grandmother. The farm had small clay buildings with tin roofs amid a spread of grass, weeds, and dirt. Chickens and goats wandered here and there. Small fields of rice were on either side. Most people living in this part of the world survive on the food they produce at home—rice, eggs, cabbage.

A group of reporters was waiting for Obama's arrival. A few dozen relatives of the Obama clan were there as well. One thin elderly man who was dressed all in white—cotton shirt, pants, and matching hat—displayed a blue-and-white OBAMA, DEMOCRAT FOR SENATE button on his chest. Most of Obama's relatives had put on their best dresses and suits.

Obama's car arrived. When Obama got out to greet his grandmother, reporters and relatives swarmed around the two. (Obama's grandmother is not actually a blood relative. She is the woman who raised his father.) Obama embraced "Granny," as she is known, while reporters and photographers and other staff crowded around, some pushing and shoving.

Obama and his grandmother strode slowly up a slight hill toward the main house, which had a new tin roof and fresh coats of blue and white paint, thanks to money Obama had sent. About halfway up the small hill, Obama stopped and realized that something was missing. "Where are my wife and children?" he asked plaintively. They had fallen behind the mass of people surrounding him. Sasha then appeared before him, and he scooped her into his arms. She looked frightened and grabbed her father tightly around the shoulders and neck. "I have you, Sasha," he said soothingly.

Reaching the main house, Obama and his grandmother disappeared inside for their first visit in nearly fourteen years. The family reunion was supposed to last nearly two and a half hours. Then Obama was to spend some time alone at his father's and grandfather's graves. But because things were so crowded and disorganized, the plans were changed. After about forty minutes Obama came out from the house and stood, arm in arm, between his eighty-three-year-old grandmother, Sarah Hussein Obama, and his half sister, Auma. They all answered questions from the press. Obama said the family had eaten porridge and chicken. Asked if his grand-mother had given him any words of wisdom, Obama answered without hesitation, "Don't trust reporters." Aides then pulled Obama away and guided him into the SUV for the trip back to the Kisumu airport and then Nairobi.

The next day Obama and his crowd of reporters and photographers visited one of the bleakest places on the planet. Kibera (pronounced KEE-bear-ah) is the largest slum in the world. Between seven hundred thousand and a million people live there, packed into just two and a half square kilometers. Most have moved there from country villages to seek better schools in Nairobi or find jobs in the large city. Many have no running water and no plumbing in their homes. Garbage is dumped into the open. Houses are made of canvas and tin. Some children do not look well fed.

Much like poor neighborhoods in the United States, Kibera is rarely visited by Kenyan politicians except at election time, when they are looking for votes. The people who lived there were gleeful to see Obama. The cars carrying Obama, his staff, and reporters could only move at a snail's pace because people had filled the streets and swarmed around the vehicles.

Outside his first event, Obama grabbed a bullhorn and raised it to his mouth, but the crowd drowned him out. He looked down, smiled and began again. "Hello!" he screamed in Luo. "Everybody in Kibera needs the same opportunities to go to school, to start businesses, to have enough to eat, to have decent clothes," he told the audience, who cheered. "I love all of you, my brothers, all of you, my sisters. I want to make sure everybody in America knows Kibera. . . . Everyone here is my brother! Everyone here is my sister! I love Kibera!"

Obama's next morning started with a tree-planting ceremony for the sake of the environment. Shovels in hand, Obama, his wife and his daughters planted an African olive tree in Freedom Park in Nairobi. That afternoon, Obama gave a speech at the University of Nairobi. Loudspeakers carried his words into courtyards and cafeterias and study rooms, where students stopped whatever they were doing to listen. He called for Kenyans—in particular, young Kenyans—to work toward ending the country's culture of corruption and politics based on loyalties to tribes rather than what is best for the country as a whole. He said that change is almost always brought about by young people rather than older adults who have gotten used to society's injustices. "Here in Kenya, it is a crisis, a crisis that is robbing an honest people of the opportunities they have fought for, the opportunity they deserve," he said.

There was warm applause during the speech. But some students said they were disappointed by his lack of specific solutions for Kenya's problems. They wanted him to be harsher with the government in power. "There are people here with so much hatred toward the government that they wanted a direct attack. They wanted him to name names," said one. "He sounded very much like a politician," another said. "He was eloquent, but it was a politician's talk."

For the next two days, Obama and his family went on safari in the Masai Mara region of Kenya. After the safari, Obama was off to Chad to speak with refugees there who had fled the civil war in nearby Sudan. He had tried to visit Sudan itself, but he has always been outspoken about the horrors occurring there, and the Sudanese government would not let him come.

Obama was frustrated because he had only ninety minutes to speak to the refugees. Their refugees' stories had to be translated from Arabic to French to English, which took a great deal of time. Obama, who had studied the Darfur situation, did not learn as much as he wanted. In his days as a community organizer, he was accustomed to listening as people on the South Side poured out their troubles for hours on end. In Chad, he didn't have that kind of time.

In a later interview, Obama said that he found the entire African journey both "wonderful" and "a little bit frustrating":

> It was a little bit frustrating [because there was] a lot of official business, a lot of pomp and circumstance, a lot of press. Which, you know, means that I can't sort of wander off and explore these countries in the way that sometimes are the best ways to learn. But, you know, obviously, the Kenya portion of the trip, in particular, evoked a response that I hadn't expected. . . . That's gratifying, in the sense that . . . when Michelle and I took that AIDS test, you know, the CDC [the Center for Disease Control] said, 'Maybe half a million people might now take an AIDS test as a consequence of you taking it.'

Upon her return to Chicago, Michelle admitted that she was "overwhelmed." "There is part of you that is embarrassed by the scene of it," she said. "Part of you just wants to say, 'Can we tame this down a little bit? Does it have to be all this? This is out of hand.' That is my instinct and I know that is his instinct too—do we really need all this?"

For Obama's half sister Auma, who now lives and works outside London, the hectic pace of the trip and the extreme enthusiasm of the Kenyans raised great concern. She fears that her brother might be headed down a path full of the same problems their father met with. She sees some similarities between the two men. After receiving an American education, her father returned to Kenya to find that his family and the Luo tribe expected great things of him. In the end Barack Sr. could not meet all those expectations and was overwhelmed by them. Obama certainly has studied his father's life and he appears to have learned from that story, Auma said. But she is still concerned. "I think Barack needs to learn from my father's mistakes," she said. "I think he is learning, but he just needs to set realistic goals for himself and set out to achieve them. Barack is like my father in that he is driven to perfection with regards to his work and he just needs to give himself a little slack. I am proud of Barack and I love him. But I worry about him."

22 LeBron Revisited

How bad can you feel when everybody is telling you that you should be president?
—A former aide of Obama's

Within weeks of his return from Africa, Barack Obama began thinking seriously about running for president in 2008. The way people in Africa had greeted him and the stories about the trip back home were very exciting. "How bad can you feel when everybody is telling you that you should be president?" asked a former aide.

Most of the stories about Obama in newspapers, magazines, and TV had been good. Even President Bush noticed the Washington love affair with Obama. "Senator Obama, I want to do a joke on you," the president told the audience at a dinner where it was traditional for politicians and reporters to tease and mock each other. "But doing a joke on you is like doing a joke on the pope. Give me something to work with. Mispronounce something." *Men's Vogue* put Obama on the cover, and in an interview the senator discussed his thoughts about becoming president. "My attitude is that you don't want to just be the president," Obama said. "You want to change the country. You want to be a great president."

Most politicians never get so much attention. Up to now, the Plan had been working nearly perfectly.

In October Obama's second book, *The Audacity of Hope: Thoughts on Reclaiming the American Dream*, hit the bookshelves. Obama launched a two-week book tour and appeared, it seemed, on every talk show. Sales boomed, and the book reached the top of *The New York Times* bestseller list. This satisfied Obama. He had asked his advisers, "What can we do to make it number one? I want to be number one."

Obama's book tour was pure madness. Thousands clamored for tickets for the events where Obama would appear. At a book signing in Portsmouth, New Hampshire, after Obama gave a speech, one listener wasn't sure if Obama was ready to lead the country, but she said his message made her an instant fan. "He's not really saying anything different than anybody else except that we should all try to work together," she said. "And it's sad to say, but that's really refreshing right now." Obama's advisers believed that his message of coming together as a country was getting through to people. "It made [running for president] something that we could no longer avoid thinking about," Robert Gibbs said.

In November, Obama and his advisers began meeting in Axelrod's office to discuss seeking the Democratic nomination for the presidency. The first person who needed to agree was Michelle. In an interview, Michelle had complained that because of her husband's work schedule, she often felt like a single mother, and she worried about Obama's connection to his daughters.

By December, Michelle had agreed, on one condition. She wanted Obama to quit smoking. He agreed. "If Barack really wants this, Michelle will support him and do what's necessary," said Cassandra Butts, Obama's friend from Harvard. "That's always been their relationship." But Michelle wanted to make sure that her children would be taken care of, even as her husband's work schedule got busier and busier. "Our kids are still really little, and what I am not ready to sacrifice is their livelihood," she said. "But . . . I am going to be the person who is providing them with the stability.

So that means my role with the kids becomes even more important. What I am not willing to do is hand my kids over to my mom and say, 'We'll see you in two years.' That's not going to happen."

Michelle also worried about the chance that someone might try to murder her husband. "I don't worry about it every day, but it's there," she said. "It only takes one person and it only takes one incident. I mean, I know history too. So it's still an issue." She made sure that her own job was secure, in case anything happened to Barack and she needed to take care of the family. "I do think about the fact that my husband is in a high-risk sort of position right now. And I need to be able to take care of myself and my kids. . . . I need to be in a position for my kids where, if they lose their father, they don't lose everything."

Considering the chances of the Democratic Party to win the White House in 2008, Obama said, "I think that over the next two years, the Democrats have to show the country that they are listening and that they are interested in crafting a set of common-sense practical solutions." With Michelle on board, with Axelrod and Gibbs getting ready, with Democrats across the country thrilled over Obama, the decision was made. In January, Obama said on his website that, in the next month, he would announce whether or not he was going to run for president.

There were people close to Obama who had some worries. No one had seen another politician get so famous so fast. It seemed that his life had been in warp speed since he first decided to run for the Senate in 2003. Would he get exhausted from the stress of running for president? "He is in fantastic shape, but I wonder about his physical stamina," said one of his advisers. "It takes just an incredible amount of physical stamina out there."

Axelrod had been asked if he thought Obama could really handle a tough race for president. "I don't know," Axelrod said. "One thing about running for president is that—and he knows this—it's like putting an X-ray machine on yourself twenty-four hours a day, because . . . at the end of the day, the American people know who you are. But with Barack, he's kind of a normal guy in a lot of ways. He likes to watch football on Sundays. He treasures his time with his kids and Michelle. I think he has an inner toughness, and that is reflected in the road he traveled to get where he is. . . . And he has, I think, struggled through a lot of challenges to make himself what he is. . . . He is a guy who was raised by a single mother who wasn't there to help all the time, because she couldn't be. And you know, he fought his way through a lot."

On a freezing February day outside the Old State Capitol in Springfield, Illinois, I stood in a grandstand filled with reporters and photographers, waiting for Barack Obama to tell the world he was running for president of the United States.

I remembered that keynote address in Boston, when I had been wondering how Obama would perform. On this day I did not wonder. I had watched him deliver speeches to blacks on Chicago's South Side, to Latinos on its Near West Side, to whites in the Illinois countryside, to people in cities across the United States and to poor villagers in remote Africa. I knew exactly what to expect.

Obama had stayed up late the night before, crafting and rehearsing these words that would tell everybody what Barack Obama believed: that all people have a lot to connect them, that if everyone would just join together behind him, he could be the one to make the world a better place.

With Michelle on his arm, Obama strode onto a long catwalk that led to a wooden podium. The handsome couple, each in a black winter overcoat, held hands as they walked forward, waving to the cheering crowd. Nearing the podium, Obama let go of Michelle's hand, and she stepped down to allow her husband to take the stage by himself. The crowd started to chant, "O-ba-ma! O-ba-ma!" The senator walked up to the podium, and I couldn't help but say to myself, "Here comes LeBron, indeed."

Afterword

Out of many, we are one. . . . While we breathe, we hope; and where we are met with cynicism and doubt and those who tell us that we can't, we will respond with that timeless creed that sums up the spirit of a people: Yes, we can.

—Barack Obama in his 2008 victory speech

After Barack Obama announced in February of 2007 that he was running for president, his first task was to win the Democratic nomination. To do that, he had to win primary elections and caucuses (where voters meet in groups to select their candidates) in state after state. State primaries and caucuses decide how many delegates will vote for each candidate when the Democratic Party holds its national convention.

There were several other Democratic candidates that Obama had to defeat first. The best known was Hillary Clinton, a senator from New York and the former first lady. Her husband, Bill Clinton, was president for eight years, from 1993 to 2001.

The two earliest Democratic contests were held in Iowa and New Hampshire. This was the first opportunity for the country to see if Obama's message had reached voters outside of Illinois.

Obama won the Iowa caucus, with more Democrats turning out than ever before in that state. Clinton won the New Hampshire primary. Other candidates gradually dropped out of the race. The first woman and the first African American to have a serious shot at the White House fought for votes all across the country.

By March of 2008, with eight states plus Puerto Rico and Guam still waiting to cast votes, most tallies put Obama ahead by a little more than 100 delegates. After a decisive victory over Clinton in North Carolina in May, it became clear that Obama would clinch the nomination.

At his party's last national convention in 2004, Obama had given the speech that made him famous. At the convention in August 2008, he became the first black candidate in United States history to be nominated for the presidency by a major party. Once a candidate is nominated by his or her party at the convention, the nominee must choose a running mate. Obama chose Senator Joseph Biden of Delaware, the chairman of the Senate Foreign Relations Committee.

Now Obama had to face Republican candidate John McCain in the general election. McCain had chosen Alaska governor Sarah Palin as his running mate. McCain's choice made waves. Opponents claimed that his choice showed poor judgment and that Palin, who had little national and international political experience, was unqualified. But Palin's grassroots message and charisma captured public attention and much media coverage. She was a rousing speaker, garnering crowd support for McCain along the campaign trail.

Three presidential debates, held on September 26, October 7, and October 15, did not seem to yield an obvious winner. Both parties felt their candidate had articulated their platform. In the polls, Obama seemed to have a clear lead over McCain, especially in key states such as Florida, Ohio, and Pennsylvania.

In late October, Obama took time from his campaign to visit his ailing grandmother, Madelyn Dunham, in Hawaii. Although some people criticized his decision, others admired Obama for showing love and devotion to the woman who had helped raise him.

A candidate must receive at least 270 electoral votes out of 538 votes to be declared the winner. On

November 4, as the polls began to close after 7 P.M. and the votes were counted, Obama emerged as the winner! In the final election results, Obama won 349 electoral votes, McCain won 162, and 27 were undecided. Obama would become the forty-fourth president of the United States, the country's first African-American president.

McCain made his concession speech from Phoenix, Arizona, after calling Obama to congratulate him on his win. Crowds had been assembling in Chicago's Grant Park, where Obama was set to spend election day. By midnight, an estimated 240,000 people had gathered together to hear President-elect Barack Hussein Obama deliver his victory speech. It would be a historic moment in American history.

Notes

Chapter 2: Dreams from His Mother

5 "Everything that is good . . . ,": Obama during Mom's Rising event in Washington, D.C., September 2006.

6 "She was extremely brilliant . . . ,": Madelyn Dunham interview with author, October 2004.

6 "Her feet never . . . ,": Dunham interview with author, October 2004.

Chapter 3: "Just Call Me Barry"

9 "I learned how to eat . . . ,": Obama, *Dreams from My Father*.

10 "I think [Indonesia] . . . ,": Obama interview on *Fresh Air*, National Public Radio, August 2004.

10 "Men take advantage . . . ,": Obama, *Dreams from My Father*.

13 "My father's absence . . . ,": Obama interview with author, December 2003.

13 "Hawaii was heaven . . . ,": Obama interview with author, August 2005.

14 "He wasn't this . . . ,": Keith Kakugawa, *Nightline*, ABC News, April 2007.

14 "He was just . . . ,": Bobby Titcomb interview with author, August 2004.

14 "In Hawaii . . . ,": Ibid.

14 "When somebody was . . . ,": Ibid.

15 "I was trying . . . ,": Obama, *Dreams from My Father*.

15 "So what I fell into . . . ,": Obama interview with author, October 2004.

17 "I recall his sincere . . . ,": Chris McLachlin interview with author, August 2004.

17 "I got into a fight . . . ,": Obama interview with author, October 2004.

17 "I recall that . . . ,": Suzanne Maurer interview with author, October 2004.

Chapter 4: The Mainland

18 "Hawaii has ideas . . . ,": Soetoro-Ng interview with author, October 2004.

19 "Although she tried . . . ,": Ibid.

20 "They weren't defined . . . ,": Obama, *Dreams from My Father*.

20 "I noticed that people . . . ,": Ibid.

21 "The schools . . . ,": Obama discussion with author, February 2004.

21 "Do you mind . . . ,": Obama, *Dreams from My Father*.

21 "It was my feeling . . . ,": Roger Boesche interview with author, June 2005.

22 "I knew that . . . ,": Obama interview with author, August 2005.

22 "Occidental was . . . ,": Obama interview with author, October 2004.

23 "I had two . . . ,": Obama interview with author, August 2005.

23 "Those two years . . . ,": Ibid.

25 "When I see . . . ,": Obama interview with author, December 2003.

Chapter 5: The Organizer

28 "All I had . . . ,": Jerry Kellman interview with author, March 2006.

28 "Jerry Kellman is . . . ,": Obama interview with author, August 2006.

28 "Barack wanted to serve . . . ," and Kellman material: Kellman interview with author, March 2006.

29 "I figured . . . ,": Obama interview with author, August 2006.

30 "It's a great book . . . ,": Obama interview with author, August 2006.

30 "It wasn't until . . . ,": Obama interview with author, October 2004.

31 "Oh, that sounds . . . ,": Jeremiah Wright interview with author, November 2006.

31 "I'm here to do . . . ,": Kellman interview with author, March 2006.

32 "In helping . . . ,": Barack Obama, "After Alinsky: Community Organizing in Illinois," *Illinois Issues*, University of Illinois at Springfield, 1990.

Chapter 6: Harvard

34 "Ain't nothing gonna . . . ,": Obama, *Dreams from My Father*.

35 "Everywhere black people . . . ,": Ibid.

35 "I just can't . . . ,": Titcomb interview with author, October 2004.

36 Laurence Tribe material: Jodi Kantor, *New York Times*, January 2007.

37 "The experience . . . ,": Cassandra Butts interview with author, December 2006.

37 "You know, whether we're . . . ,": Ibid.

38 "just ridiculously . . . ,": Brad Berenson quoted in "In Law School," Kantor, *New York Times*, January 2007.

38 "Barack made no . . . ,": Berenson interview with author, January 2007.

39 "I had to . . . ,": Obama interview with author, October 2004.

39–40 "He wanted to be mayor . . . ,": Butts interview with author, December 2006.

Chapter 7: Sweet Home Chicago

42 "He sounded too good . . . ," and "I thought . . . ,": Michelle Obama interview with author, January 2004.

43 "We always felt . . . ,": Craig Robinson interview with author, November 2005.

44 "I sometimes . . . ,": Michelle Obama interview with author, January 2004.

45 "Barack's game . . . ,": Robinson interview with author, November 2005.

45 "Barack was like . . . ,": Ibid.

46 "I told him . . . ,": Michelle Obama interview with author, January 2004.

47 "There are times . . . ,": Obama interview with author, October 2004.

47 "Fact Guy . . . ,": Michelle Obama interview with author, January 2004.

48 "The courts are . . . ,": Obama interview with author, October 2004.

Chapter 8: Politics

51 "People are hungry. . . ,": Obama quoted by Hank De Zutter in the *Chicago Reader*, December 1995.

51 "He wants to . . . ,": Dan Shomon interview with author, January 2005.

52 "looked flabbergasted . . . ,": Ibid.

52–53 "It was just a great . . . ,": Ibid.

53 "I understand . . . ,": Obama discussion with author, August 2004.

Chapter 9: The Legislator

54 "It wasn't like . . . ,": Shomon interview with author, January 2005.

54 "Barack is . . . ,": Rich Miller quoted in "How Obama Learned to Be a Natural," Edward McClelland, *Salon.com*, February 2007.

55 "Emil is driven . . . ,": Obama discussion with author, February 2004.

55 "I am blessed . . . ,": Emil Jones Jr. discussion with author, February 2004.

56 "I always found . . . ,": Joe Birkett discussion with author, October 2006.

56 "The most important . . . ,": Obama interview with author, September 2004.

56 "Members of both . . . ,": Kirk Dillard interview with author, September 2004.

57 "It's never been . . . ,": Obama interview with author, October 2004.

58 "I cannot sacrifice . . . ,": Obama in press conference, January 2000.

58 "Less than halfway . . . ,": Obama, *The Audacity of Hope*.

59 "Bobby just ain't . . . ,": Obama interview with author, October 2004.

59 "I was broke . . . ,": Obama press interviews in Boston, July 2004.

60 "I told Barack . . . ,": Shomon interview with author, January 2005.

Chapter 10: The Candidate

61–62 "The big issue . . . ," and "Whatever . . . ,": Michelle Obama interview with author, December 2006.

62 "So I told Dan . . . ,": Obama interview with author, December 2004.

63 "Barack says he wants . . . ," and "He convinced us . . . ,":

Marty Nesbitt interview with author, October 2005.

63 "We were pulling . . . ,": David Axelrod discussion with author, December 2004.

64 "My name should . . . ,": Obama from author interview with Wright, November 2006.

65–66 "I didn't grow up . . . ,": Obama interview with author, December 2004.

Chapter 11: The Consultant

68 "I just wanted to go . . . ,": Axelrod interview with the author, June 2005.

70 "When he speaks . . . ,": Bettylu Saltzman interview with author, April 2005.

71 "I knew that this . . . ,": Obama interview with author, December 2004.

72 "That's the speech . . . ,": Obama interview with author, August 2006.

73 "My involvement was . . . ,": Axelrod interview with author, December 2004.

Chapter 12: The Race Factor

75 Jones-Obama conversation: Jones interview with author, January 2007.

76 "This is the . . . ,": Obama interview with author, December 2004.

76–77 "When I was . . . ,": Obama interview with author, December 2003.

77–78 "This Senate thing . . . ,": Shomon in interview with author, January 2005.

78 Jim Cauley quotes: Jim Cauley interview with author, December 2004.

79 "Some are whispering . . . ,": *Chicago Sun-Times*, Laura Washington column, September 2003.

80 "I am not running . . . ,": Obama at Mars Hill Baptist Church, Chicago, November 2003.

82 "It's like that . . . ,": Michelle Obama interview with author, August 2005.

Chapter 13: The Small Screen

84 "Don't you think . . . ,": from Illinois political consultant discussion with author, June 2005.

85 "Barack was concerned . . . ,": Axelrod interview with author, August 2005.

85 "I knew Dan Hynes . . . ,": Illinois politico discussion with author, August 2005.

86 "My general attitude . . . ,": Obama interview with author, December 2004.

87 "I am my . . . ,": Obama in various campaign speeches, 2003–2004.

87–88 Campaign ads courtesy of David Axelrod.

88 "Barack is extremely intelligent . . . ,": Axelrod interview with author, March 2004.

89 "Obama is on fire": Jason Erkes discussion with author, March 2004.

Chapter 14: A Victory

91 "We have all . . . ,": Cauley discussion with author, March 2004.

91 *Tribune* story reference: Mendell/Chase, "Candidate Without Faults Is a Rarity," *Chicago Tribune*, March 2004.

92 "I chewed . . . ,": Obama discussion with author, March 2004.

92 "He did . . . ,": Axelrod discussion with author, March 2004.

94 "Well, you are . . . ,": Valerie Jarrett conversation recounted to author, May 2005.

94 "He's really pretty excited…,": Michelle Obama quoted in Eric Zorn column, *Chicago Tribune*, March 2004.

94 "The most surprising . . . ,": Axelrod interview with author, June 2005.

95 "Truthfully, it feels . . . ,": Leslie Corbett, quoted in "Obama Enters New Ring," *Chicago Tribune*, Mendell/Jon Yates, March 2004.

95 "When I first . . . ,": Deborah Landis interview with author, March 2004.

95 "At its best . . . ,": Obama victory speech, Chicago, March 2004.

Chapter 15: The Ryan Files

98 "Barack was . . . ,": Cauley discussion with author, April 2004.

98 "Robert is . . . ,": former Obama aide discussion with author, October 2006.

100 "I've tried to make . . . ,": Obama interview with author, June 2004.

100 "Barack just killed . . . ,": Nate Tamarin interview with author, December 2004.

101 "It came out . . . ,": Obama interview with author, August 2005.

Chapter 16: The Speech

102–103 Obama's convention day material: David Mendell, adapted from "Obama Finding Himself Flush with Media Attention," *Chicago Tribune*, July 28, 2004.

103 "You're the . . . ,": Bob Schieffer conversation with Obama, Boston, July 2004.

104 "I wasn't . . . ,": Obama at press conference, Boston, July 2004.

104 "I can't . . . ,": Obama speech to League of Conservation Voters, Boston, July 2004.

105 "Even that last try . . . ,": practice speech observer conversation with author, July 2006.

105–108 various DNC speech quotes: Obama, Boston, July 2004.

106 "Of all . . . ,": Axelrod interview with author, December 2004.

108 "When I looked . . . ,": Julian Green conversation

with author, March 2005.

108 "I guess . . . ,": Obama, as recounted by Green to author, March 2005.

Chapter 17: Back to Illinois

110 "I don't want . . . ,": Cauley, Obama quote recounted to author, August 2004.

111 "Apparently . . . ,": Obama to audience in Kewanee, Illinois, August 2004.

111–112 "I vote for . . . ,": David Bramson interview with author, August 2004.

112 "I can't go . . . ,": Dick Durbin conversation with Obama, August 2004.

112 "When we send . . . ,": Obama to audience in Quincy, Illinois, August 2004.

113 "Someone is going . . . ,": Mike Daly conversation with campaign aides, August 2004.

113 "When are we . . . ,": Obama conversation with Michelle Obama, August 2004.

115 "Barack thinks . . . ,": Cauley conversation with author, September 2004.

115 "You know, Barack . . . ,": Axelrod, recounted by Obama in conversation with author, September 2004.

116 "I can't believe . . . ,": Obama, recounted to author by campaign aide, August 2004.

116 "I am not looking . . . ,": Obama, recounted by Cauley

during interview with author, December 2004.

Chapter 18: The Senator

117 "Congratulations" anecdote: conversation between the Obamas, January 2005.

118 "I'm not a . . . ,": Obama conversation with Jesse Jackson Sr., January 2005.

118 "We are going . . . ,": Obama to supporters in Washington, D.C., January 2005.

120 "I'm writing . . . ,": Obama conversation with author, April 2005.

120 "Does he . . . ,": Rahm Emanuel discussion with author, May 2005.

121 "has no time . . . ,": Shomon conversation with author, April 2006.

121 "I think that. . . ,": Obama interview with author, December 2006.

121 "And he just . . . ,": Chris Lu interview with author, December 2006.

122–123 Knox College speech quotes: Obama to audience at college, June 2005.

124–125 Katrina quotes: Obama on *This Week with George Stephanopoulos*, ABC News, September 2005.

125 "I was jailed . . . ,": Jackson quote: interview with author, June 2006.

125–126 "Not everybody's . . . ,": Obama interview with author, December 2005.

139 "Oh my goodness . . . ,": Michelle Obama conversation with author, August 2006.

140 "He is my . . . ,": Gregory Ochieng interview with author, August 2006.

141 "Part of my role . . . ," and subsequent Obama quotes: Obama at a press conference, August 2006.

142 "Kenya is not my . . . ,": Obama at a press conference, August 2006.

Chapter 21: Siaya: A Father's Home

144 "The last time . . . ,": Obama to reporters, August 2006.

145 "Stop pushing . . . ,": Obama to a crowd at a hospital, August 2006.

146 "It's all a bit . . . ,": Michelle Obama discussion with reporters, August 2006.

147 "Hopefully, I can . . . ,": Obama in a school dedication ceremony, August 2006.

147–149 "As I was driving . . . ,": Obama speech to Siaya political gathering, August 2006.

151 "Don't trust . . . ,": Obama to reporters outside grandmother's house, August 2006.

152 "Hello . . . ;": Obama to a crowd in Kibera, August 2006.

153 "Here in Kenya . . . ,": Obama in a speech at University of Nairobi, August 2006.

153 "There are people . . . ,": Onyango interview with

author, August 2006.

154–155 "It was a little . . . ,": Obama interview with author, December 2006.

155 "There is part . . . ,": Michelle Obama interview with author, December 2006.

155 "I think Barack . . . ,": Auma Obama interview with author, August 2006.

Chapter 22: LeBron Revisited

157 "How bad . . . ,": Tamarin conversation with author, October 2006.

158 "My attitude is . . . ,": Jacob Weisberg, "Barack Obama: The Path to Power," *Men's Vogue*, September 2006.

158–159 "He's not really . . . ,": Penny Reynolds interview with author, December 2006.

159 "It made [running] . . . ,": Gibbs interview with author, May 2007.

159 "If Barack . . . ,": Butts interview with author, December 2006.

159 "Our kids . . . ," and subsequent quotes: Michelle Obama interview with author, December 2006.

160 "I think . . . ,": Obama interview with author, December 2006.

161 "He is in fantastic . . . ,": Pete Giangreco interview with author, January 2007.

161 "I don't know . . . ,": Axelrod interview with author, December 2006.